BUDMO!

ANNA VOLOSHYNA

BUDMO!

Recipes from a Ukranian Kitchen

RIZZOLI
NEW YORK

New York Paris London Milan

CONTENTS

...⬦...

PICKLES, SAUCES, AND DRINKS

DESSERTS

Introduction

—◦ Вступ

I was lucky to be born and raised in Ukraine, the second-largest country in Europe and home to many vital and longstanding cultural and culinary traditions. Our two primary languages are Ukrainian and Russian, which are both part of the eastern branch of the Slavic language family, which means we share many similar words. (The word *Ukraine* comes from the Slavic word *kraj*, which means "region" or "country" as well as "borderland.")

The country lies at the very heart of Eastern Europe, at the crossroads of Western Europe, Russia, and Asia, which has proved both a blessing and a curse. In the thirteenth century, this strategically located land was stormed by the Mongols. Later it would be occupied, split, and ruled by various powers, including the Polish-Lithuanian Commonwealth, Austria-Hungary, the Ottoman Empire, the Tsardom of Russia, and finally the USSR. Every invasion left its mark on the everyday life and the cuisine of the country.

The invaders were drawn not only by location, but also by the varied and productive terrain. The majority of Ukraine, especially the central and southern parts, consists of steppes (temperate grasslands) that are famous for their rich black soil, or *chernozem*. Because of that fertile landscape, Ukraine is known as the "breadbasket of Europe," and wheat, rye, barley, and other grains are central to the country's cuisine. So, too, are vegetable staples like potatoes, beets, cabbage, and mushrooms. They all go into an array of national specialties, such as borscht, *varenyky* (dumplings), *pampushky* (small yeasted rolls), and stuffed cabbage.

Regional cuisines, shaped by local traditions and their geographical position, employ their own signature take on various ingredients, cooking styles, and preserving techniques, turning out unique flavors and signature dishes. For example, in Mykolaiv Oblast, which is in southern Ukraine, cheese *varenyky* typically have a sweet filling and only rarely a savory one. But in western Ukraine, the flavor profile is completely opposite: tangy, savory *syr* (fresh cheese) is one of the most popular fillings for *varenyk*y and the plate is finished with crispy bits of fried pork belly (*skvarky*) and plenty of sour cream.

In fact, western Ukraine is one of the country's most recognizable culinary regions. It shares not only borders with Poland, Hungary, Slovakia, and Moldova but also ingredients and similar dishes. One of my favorite foods of the region is *bryndza*, a splendid sheep's milk cheese that originates with the Hutsuls, a small ethnic group at home in the Carpathian Mountains. The cheese, which is produced from the milk of sheep grazed on highland meadows, is briny, tangy, crumbly, and slightly moist. It's often served on top of *banosh*, creamy Hutsul polenta, with sprigs of aromatic herbs and sliced fresh vegetables. In the other parts of Ukraine, *bryndza* is made from cow's milk and has a distinctly different flavor and a firmer, springier texture.

The central and northern areas of the country have a little bit of everything. The most famous dishes are potatoes and meat braised in a clay pot, the Polish cabbage stew *bigos*, and latke-like potato pancakes called *deruny* (also known as *kremzlyky*), which are often served with a luscious sour cream sauce laced with local mushrooms. Another dish common to this part of Ukraine—and to neighboring Poland—is red borscht made with bright and fizzy beet *kvass*, just one of the many versions of this iconic soup found throughout the country.

Growing up in Ukraine, I was surrounded by delicious food and lively family feasts celebrating every possible occasion, from a birthday to a three-day outdoor wedding to Old New Year (Orthodox New Year). These occasions were always bustling and loud, the dishes were home cooked, and the ingredients came straight from my grandma's garden or the local *bazaar* (farmers' market). No one went to restaurants because after the collapse of the USSR in 1991, there weren't a lot of them. Moreover, the ones that did exist simply weren't good. All meals for all occasions were cooked and served by female home cooks. And I was lucky to grow up among those women who could single-handedly create a ten-course meal for twelve people without any professional training or fancy equipment. They could juggle half a dozen pots and pans without skipping a beat. I watched them and eagerly tried to remember every detail. The food was always served family-style, with thick slices of dark rye bread and chilled vodka, which set the mood for countless toasts and long conversations.

I titled this cookbook *Budmo*, which means "let us be"—the English equivalent of "cheers"—because it is my favorite Ukrainian word and signals a celebration. Whenever I hear it, I know there will be delicious food, blazing drinks, and countless toasts. This word is fierce and vigorous—a perfect embodiment of Eastern European cuisine.

A TANGLED HISTORY

The term *Eastern European* is a challenge to define. Some people view the region geographically—the countries on the European continent between Western Europe and Asia—while others prefer a geopolitical definition—all the European countries formerly ruled by the Soviet Union. Cultural anthropologists typically apply yet another set of dividing lines, though they sometimes disagree among themselves. Regardless of which "map" one favors, however, everyone agrees that the countries that make up this mass of shifting borders are distinct from one another and at the same time have much in common. It is tricky to understand, even for me, as someone who lived in that melting pot for most of my life.

Although the region has undergone varying degrees of turmoil over many centuries due to cultural and ethnic differences, economic disparity, and conflicting religious beliefs, the establishment of the Soviet Union in 1922 launched a particularly concentrated period of upheaval. With the end of Soviet rule in late 1991, many of the countries that had made up the so-called Eastern Bloc tried to disassociate themselves from their former alliance.

This long history has led to a very fluid list of Eastern European countries today. According to the United Nations Statistics Division, Eastern Europe includes Bulgaria, the Czech Republic, Hungary, Poland, Romania, and Slovakia, as well as Ukraine, Belarus, Moldova, and the Russian Federation. All of them except Romania and Hungary are also considered part of the Slavic ethnolinguistic group. Other sources add the Baltic republics of Estonia, Latvia, and Lithuania and the Transcaucasian countries of Armenia, Azerbaijan, and Georgia to the list. I agree with this more inclusive group because all of these countries were heavily influenced by the Soviet regime and share a common history, language (Russian), and many social and culinary traditions.

In its pursuit of building a "brave new world," the Soviet Communist Party tried to abolish the cultural

identity of its republics with its mighty sickle and hammer. That included integrating their diverse national tables into a single new, uniform Soviet cuisine, with most of the "approved" dishes simplifications of French, Russian, Ukrainian, and Georgian recipes. Consequently, the distinctive culinary characteristics of the Soviet republics and their various ethnic groups were almost completely erased. Nearly all of the restaurants in the USSR were replaced by identical government-run canteens (*stolovyye*) that served indistinguishable menus prepared from limited and often scarce produce, meats, and other ingredients. The rise of the *stolovaya* was a dark time in the region's culinary history, and many national cuisines are still recovering.

After the dissolution of the Soviet Union, the former republics actively began to rebuild their own identities, growing detached from one another. But their common history and cultural heritage are forever intertwined. It is especially pronounced in the kitchen: Eastern European cuisine is easily recognizable and is seldom mistaken for other national cuisines. In her seminal work, *The Ethnic Food Lover's Companion*, Eve Zibart writes, "With the fall of the communism and the economic reconstruction of Eastern Europe, we can hope for a revival of not merely classic Russian and Polish dishes but Hungarian, Romanian, Czech, Bulgarian, or Ukrainian ones as well. These are substantial cuisines, meaty, rooty, smoky—part comfort food, part extravagance." I couldn't agree more. Call me biased, but for me, Eastern Europe is one of the most exciting, multilayered—and often overlooked—culinary regions in the world.

MY CULINARY MEMORIES

I grew up in the small town of Snihurivka, which lies in the very south of Ukraine between the port cities of Kherson and Mykolaiv and about 120 miles from historic Odessa. The surrounding area is a land of abundance, with vast stretches of sunflower fields, flourishing fruit orchards, and the long, winding Dnieper River teeming with fish. In Ukraine, unlike in the San Francisco Bay Area where I now live, we have all four seasons, with long, hot summers and frosty winters. These dramatic changes in temperature have had a great impact on the local cuisine. With at least five months of the year too cold to cultivate crops or even a household vegetable garden, we learned how to cherish every young spring zucchini, preserve summertime's sweet apricots, and ferment end-of-the-season ripe tomatoes for the winter table. From an early age, I knew to enjoy fruits and vegetables while they are in their prime and to conserve them for when the weather turned cold.

Every Saturday and Sunday morning, my mom and I, armed with a couple of woven willow baskets, would go to a local farmers' market to buy fresh produce and other foods for the whole week. We bought dairy from Tanya, our trusted source for *smetana (*sour cream), milk, and all kinds of fresh cheeses, and we usually got our meat from Vova and Marina, a family from a nearby village who had a small farm with pigs and chickens. I still remember Vova's amazing kielbasa twisted into twelve-inch rings and hanging from the very top of his small stand. It smelled of cherrywood smoke, fresh garlic, and clove.

To buy the rest of what we needed, we would go to every single vendor, sometimes twice, smelling and tasting everything, comparing prices, and bargaining with the sellers for whatever we wanted to purchase. At the Ukrainian *bazaar*, you never pay the full price. You need to haggle for every item, even if it is just a small bunch of parsley. This is an entertaining game both for the buyer and the seller. My mom and grandma are bargaining pros, and they always get the best deals. Unfortunately, I did not inherit that skill from them—not that I could use it at a California farmers' market!

When we returned home from the *bazaar*, my mom would make a lavish breakfast with some of the foods that we had bought that day. When I was little, I would sit in the kitchen quietly, observing her moving quickly and nimbly from the fridge to the stove, making breakfast for the whole family. Since my sister was even younger than I, and my father would eat whatever my mom cooked, she would let me choose the breakfast dishes for everyone. When I craved something sweet, I would usually request *syrnyky* (fried cheese fritters) topped with apricot jam. For the savory choice, I would ask for sunny-side up eggs cooked with kielbasa or pork belly, served with a slab of homemade bread and a simple tomato salad dressed with a dollop of *smetana*. I was not a picky eater, and I always knew exactly what I wanted to eat that morning. Surprisingly, very little has changed since then.

THE UKRAINIAN KITCHEN

In Ukraine, just like in pretty much any Eastern European country, a family's life is centered in the kitchen. People not only cook and eat there but also discuss family business and politics and share their hopes and dreams over a shot of liquor. It is the place where my happiest food memories were born. I have enjoyed being around food since I was a kid. Whether it was helping my grandma arrange her freshly made sour-cherry *varenyky*, or waiting for my mom to serve her signature golden, thick, fluffy *oladky* (pancakes), I was always there, ready to help and to taste.

To me, everything was important: the smell, the texture, the sound. An aroma coming from the oven would indicate that the roasted pork shank was cooking as planned. The skin would start changing its color from pale pink to a golden brown, and the meat would become so tender it could be sliced with a spoon. The texture of the *varenyk* dough had to be pliable and elastic to the touch, never stiff. The sound of borscht bubbling vigorously on the stove signaled it was time to lower the heat and send the garlicky *pampushky* to the oven. Those memories are incredibly intense, and even now, they bring back the vibrant flavors and heady aromas of my childhood, giving me a feeling of eternal happiness.

I carried those food memories with me to California and brought them to life by sharing my favorite dishes with others. Cooking became my way of telling new friends about my family and the culture I grew up in. It is how I was able to connect with people and nurture relationships that have continued to grow over the years.

Sharing food with others in California came to me naturally, as it is a time-honored Eastern European tradition that I saw every day as a child. In Ukraine, even if guests arrived unannounced, a good hostess would always set the table with a couple of hearty dishes, homemade pickles, and some hard liquor— usually vodka in large cities or fiery *samogon* (moonshine) in villages. Cooking and eating together are deeply rooted in the culture. Typically, while family matriarchs teach kids how to make the family recipes, they tell them stories from their youth. It is a beautiful exchange between generations that ensures the culture will be preserved.

ABOUT THIS BOOK

I have tried to capture the complex and delicious story of Eastern European food and the spirit of the exuberant get-togethers I grew up with in *Budmo!*, where traditional Soviet-era dishes like *salat Olivye* (the famous New Year's potato salad) are interlaced with plump Ukrainian *varenyky*, savory Russian *pelmeni*, and crispy Tatar *chebureki* (meat-stuffed hand pies). I hope that you will be encouraged to create your own multicultural meals, where perhaps a delicious platter of Uzbek *plov* (rice) with whole quail, caramelized garlic, and large chunks of tender meat is served with flavorful eggplant rolls and delightful beet *pkhali* (walnut spread), two specialties of Georgia. Despite the fact that all of these dishes come from very different parts of the former USSR, they long ago became an important part of the Eastern European culinary culture—beloved and relished outside their original borders.

I feel incredibly fortunate to have the opportunity to bring the iconic flavors and aromas from all the corners of Eastern Europe to the rest of the world, share memories, and tell stories through my dishes. Before the pandemic, I was happy to host my pop-up dinners in San Francisco and welcome strangers around the large communal table. As we look to the future, I anticipate those heartwarming events even more. It's a true joy to see diners' reactions when they taste the sweet-and-sour pickled tomatoes I make using my mom's recipe, or tear apart oozy *khachapuri* (Georgian flatbread), something they have never tried before. Countless conversations are born and new friendships are forged at every dinner. Whether it's a single diner, a couple, or a group of friends celebrating a birthday, everyone is welcome at my table.

As a young cook who moved from Ukraine to California at the age of twenty-one, I feel it's my duty to keep these dishes alive, tell their stories, and share my culture. In this cookbook, you will find recipes that are perfect for large family gatherings, lazy weekend brunches, and quiet weeknight dinners. Some recipes are very traditional and were born from my childhood memories, but most are my modern interpretations of beloved classics. All of them are meant to make you fall in love with new flavors and aromas and expand your cooking horizons. Gather around your own table and raise a glass to the spirit of *Budmo!*

My Pantry
Комора

Cooking Eastern European food does not require any exotic components or myriad spices. With a few exceptions, you can find most of these ingredients in any well-stocked grocery store; others are available in Eastern European, Armenian, or Russian markets or can be purchased online.

BAY LEAF
Dried bay leaf is an essential component for Slavic and Caucasus soups, stews, and all sorts of pickles. Its herbaceous aroma complements both meat and vegetable dishes. I always keep a small jar of dried bay leaves in my pantry and get a new supply every six months. Like most spices, bay leaf loses its mojo after half a year on the shelf.

BUCKWHEAT
If Slavs had to choose one type of cereal to eat for the rest of their lives, it would certainly be buckwheat. It makes a wonderfully hearty kasha—or porridge—especially when served with fried mushrooms and onions. In Eastern Europe, toasted buckwheat is preferred, as toasting gives it a beautiful dark brown color and deep earthy flavor. You can get buckwheat at any Eastern European market and in some well-stocked supermarkets. The widely available Bob's Red Mill brand sells organic buckwheat, which it labels "kasha."

DILL
Fresh dill is without a doubt the most popular herb in Slavic cuisine. If you've ever had a meal in an Eastern European restaurant, you have probably noticed that the kitchen generously tops almost every savory dish with dill. In Ukraine, cooks love this herb so much that they pair it with everything: fresh young dill is for salads and garnishes, fresh mature dill with seeds is for pickling and brining, and dried dill is for flavoring winter stews and braises.

GARLIC
It is hard to overestimate the importance of garlic in Eastern European cuisine. I rely on it a lot in my everyday cooking and can go into full panic mode when I run out of it. As you'll learn from this book, Slavic food is very straightforward and centered around local ingredients and simple flavor combinations. We rarely use more than two spices in a single dish. That's because historically foreign spices were too costly for common people, so they never made their way into daily cooking. But there was always an abundance of garlic, so it turns up often in dishes. It adds life, brightness, and much-needed complexity to the Slavic table.

HONEY
I regularly have three types of honey in my pantry. One is local, from Napa or Sonoma; it is typically light and floral, such as wildflower, acacia, orange blossom, or clover. That one I use for my everyday cooking as a substitute for sugar, for adding extra flavor, and, of course, for making my favorite honey cake (page 210). The second type is buckwheat honey, which is deep, dark, and almost overwhelmingly complex. I add just a tiny bit of it to my dishes or drinks for a little extra oomph. And last but not least is crystallized raw honey, which I use when I make creamed honey for barley blini (page 143). I love how the simple act of whipping crystallized and liquid honey together gives the two ingredients an unexpected new form.

HORSERADISH

If you like everything spicy and warming, horseradish is a perfect ingredient for you. In Ukraine, cooks use both the root and the leaves of the horseradish plant. The leaves add an incredible aroma to fermented vegetables and are one of the key flavor components in our famous sour cucumbers. The root is usually grated and used in hot sauces, such as Red Ajika (page 171) and Beet and Horseradish Hot Sauce (page 167). Horseradish root is also used to make the popular vodka infusion known as *khrenovukha* (page 182), which is so powerful that after one shot your brain will feel like it is doing somersaults.

PICKLES

Pickled and fermented fruits and vegetables are part of the Slavic culinary DNA. We pickle everything from mushrooms and whole apples to gooseberries. These sour, tangy, crunchy, fizzy tidbits make an excellent pairing for ice-cold vodka. If you've never been to an Eastern European store, hunting for some cool pickles is the perfect excuse for your first visit.

PORK BELLY

I always keep a decent slab of pork belly in my freezer, just like my mom does. It is such a flavorful and versatile piece of meat, and I have a few recipes in this book to prove it to you.

RYE BREAD

It's hard to imagine Slavic cuisine without this dark, dense, and incredibly delicious bread. When I call for rye bread in this book, I mean the one that looks like a dark brown brick topped with coriander and caraway seeds. Look for it at your local Scandinavian or Jewish bakery or ask for dark Lithuanian rye in an Eastern European grocery store.

SALMON ROE

Maybe it is just a Slavic thing, but I feel like there is something incredibly festive and lavish about spreading glimmering coral pearls of salmon roe on a freshly made blini or piping-hot *lángos* (page 119). I always have a jar of salmon roe in my fridge just in case I feel like it's time to celebrate life.

SOUR CREAM

We call it *smetana* in Ukraine. Sour cream is the must-have ingredient for this book, especially if you're planning to make borscht. In our family, eating borscht without *smetana* is considered a crime against borscht. I'm only half joking. You can find sour cream in almost any grocery store. My personal favorite is from Straus Family Creamery, based in Marin County.

SUNFLOWER OIL

Sunflower oil is the heart and soul of Ukrainian cooking. Most of the recipes in this book call for refined sunflower oil, which is pale yellow and has a very subtle sunflower flavor. This versatile oil, which is referred to simply as sunflower oil in my recipes, can be used for every cooking temperature, from low to extremely high. Refined sunflower oil is sold in almost every supermarket these days, though in a pinch, you can substitute canola oil or grapeseed oil.

Some recipes call for unrefined (cold-pressed) sunflower oil, which is a beautiful deep amber and has a lovely, distinctive flavor of toasted sunflower seeds. This oil is used primarily for dressing salads or as a finishing oil. It can be purchased online or at a Slavic food market.

SYR (TVOROG)

Syr is the Ukrainian name for *tvorog* cheese, and in Ukraine, the two words are used interchangeably. It is a fresh curd Eastern European cheese similar to quark and *fromage blanc*. I use it in quite a few recipes in this book and highly recommend that you make it from scratch (page 174). But you can also search for it in the dairy section in Eastern European grocery stores, where it will most likely be labeled *twaróg*, the Polish spelling.

TOMATO PASTE

Tomato paste is an essential ingredient of the Ukrainian kitchen, where it is a wonderful addition to soups, sauces, and stews. Just a tablespoon or so will deepen the flavor of a braise, add lacking acidity to borscht, or merge the ingredients in a meat stock.

VODKA

In Ukraine, we do not produce good wine, but we do know how to make good vodka. I am not a vodka drinker myself, but I use it to make all types of infusions, including delicious *nastoyanka* (page 179). I also add a dash of vodka to the dough for my *chebureki* to make it light and bubbly. This trick works like magic. If you are cooking from this book and inviting your friends over, you have to drink at least one shot of vodka with food to get an authentic experience. One thing I can tell you for sure, if you have a bottle of vodka in your freezer, you will never have a dull party in your house. *Budmo!*

Glossary

⸻ Словник

Although Ukrainian has many similarities with Russian, Polish, Slovak, and other Eastern European languages from the same language group, it has its own unique words and spellings. I have assembled this list of the most useful and sometimes most confusing Ukrainian culinary terms to avoid misunderstanding.

BAZAAR (farmers' market) In Ukraine, the *bazaar* is the source of the freshest, most amazing local produce. These markets are usually held on weekends, and you can buy not only fresh fruits and vegetables but also anything from a pig's head to local honey to homemade pickles made by a cute Ukrainian *babushka*. It's a fun place for a culinary tour and even better for a food tasting.

BUDMO (cheers) When we drink in Ukraine, instead of saying cheers, we say *budmo*, which literally means "let us be." It is a compelling word that contains a wish for good health, prosperity, and the enjoyment of being present in the moment.

KASHA (cereal or grain porridge) In the United States, when people talk about kasha, they are referring to raw or cooked buckwheat. In Eastern European countries, kasha is a sweet or savory porridge made from nearly any grain or cereal.

NASTOYANKA (vodka infusion) Slavs are notorious vodka drinkers, and we love infusing it with everything that grows under the sun. There are countless *nastoyanka* types in Ukraine, but my personal favorites are fierce horseradish *khrenovykha* (page 182) and lush apple *nastoyanka* (page 179).

POSYDEN'KY (small gathering) This is a somewhat vague term, but from my viewpoint, any gathering that includes up to eight people is a *posyden'ky* and anything bigger than that is a feast. Most of the time, a *posyden'ky* starts in the late afternoon. First, small bites and salads are served, next the meal progresses into main dishes and sides, and then it ends with tea, coffee, and sweets. And, of course, the flow is constantly interrupted with toasts and drinks.

PYRIG (pie) Even though *pyrig* is translated as "pie," it is actually used for a wide range of pastry types, including the pies everyone knows and loves in the United States. Traditional Ukrainian *pyrig* is usually made with yeasted dough, has a sweet or savory filling, and is baked until it develops a deep golden, glossy crust.

PYRIZHKY (fried or baked yeasted pastries) These pastries, which are traditionally quite small, are stuffed with a cooked or raw filling, shaped into oval patties, and then fried in sunflower oil or baked.

SMACHNOGO (bon appétit) *Smachno* in Ukrainian means "delicious." When people say *smachnogo*, they are literally wishing you a very tasty meal. I hope you will say this word many times when you cook dishes from this book.

SUPRA (Georgian feast) This is a Georgian word, not a Ukrainian word, but because I refer to it a few times in this book, I decided to include it here in this otherwise Ukrainian glossary. A *supra* is a traditional Georgian feast and is, in my opinion,

the most lavish and bountiful culinary experience Eastern Europe offers. It is always led by a *tamada* (a toast maker), who orchestrates the feast and keeps the mood light and the wine flowing.

VARENYKY (dumplings aka pierogi; *varenyk* is singular) These traditional Ukrainian dumplings are the less famous twin brother of Polish pierogi. The symbolic meaning of *varenyk* traces its roots to the era of Slavic paganism. Back then, these half-moon-shaped dumplings symbolized the crescent moon and fertility. *Varenyky* usually have a slightly different stuffing than pierogi. Among the traditional fillings are sweet or savory *syr*, braised cabbage, mashed potatoes, sour cherries, and poppy seeds.

ZAKUSKY (appetizers; *zakuska* is singular) These are Slavic small bites, cold cuts, and pickles served with vodka. In Ukraine, a typical spread includes thinly sliced *salo* (salt- or brine-cured pork fat), rye bread canapés, pickled herring, and fermented vegetables.

STARTERS, SALADS, AND SPREADS

ЗАКУСКИ

IN EASTERN EUROPEAN COUNTRIES, there is a certain flow you need to keep in mind when it comes to feasting. The dishes are served from cold to hot and from lighter to heartier. For example, savory pastries like *pyrizhky* and various dumplings often come halfway through the meal or together with the soup. But the main rule to follow is that an abundant table is an absolute must, even if you host just a few close friends.

All kinds of salads, spreads, cold cuts, cured meats, and fish are called a *zakuska*, which simply means "appetizer." *Zakuska* arrive at the beginning of the meal to arouse appetites and accompany first toasts. Some *zakyska*, especially various cold cuts and briny pickles,

stay on the table throughout the whole meal for following every shot. Those small, flavorful bites are perfect for mellowing out fiery *horilka* (vodka) or other hard liquors. Don't forget to say "*Budmo!*" right before you drink your first shot.

In this chapter, I put together my favorite *zakuska* recipes. Some dishes, such as Black Sea Pickled Mussels and Famous Odessa Forshmak, are native to southern Ukraine, where I grew up. Others, like Georgian Eggplant Rolls and Vegetarian Russian Potato Salad, come from former USSR republics. Mix and match the dishes on these pages as you like to create a colorful spread to launch a bountiful meal.

Roasted Peppers

with Tvorog Cheese and Herbs

Запечені перці

1 pound mini sweet bell peppers or gypsy bell peppers

8 ounces tvorog cheese, homemade (page 174) or store-bought, or feta cheese

¼ cup plain full-fat Greek yogurt

1 cup chopped mixed fresh herbs (such as mint, tarragon, dill, and flat-leaf parsley)

2 garlic cloves, minced

Salt and freshly ground black pepper

2 tablespoons extra-virgin olive oil

Beautiful charred peppers always remind me of summer in Ukraine and of our countless family picnics. My mom would make her famous zesty Tvorog Herby Spread (page 58), which was packed with vibrant flavors from aromatic herbs and garlic. Of course, I would be the one constantly slathering the cheese on a slice of rye bread and topping it with a stack of fire-roasted sweet Bulgarian peppers (similar to bell peppers). The memories of those midsummer feasts inspired me to create this dish: small, soft, delicate bell peppers stuffed with my favorite childhood treat.

Preheat the oven to 500°F. Line a large sheet pan with aluminum foil.

Arrange the peppers in a single layer on the prepared pan and roast, turning them once or twice, until soft, wrinkly, and evenly blackened on all sides, about 20 minutes. Transfer the peppers to a large bowl, cover the bowl with plastic wrap, and leave to steam and loosen the skin, 10 to 15 minutes. When the peppers are cool enough to handle but still warm, peel off and discard the skin.

In a medium bowl, combine the cheese, yogurt, herbs, and garlic and, using a stiff rubber spatula, mix well to form a smooth paste. Season to taste with salt and pepper.

Using a small, sharp knife, carefully make a lengthwise slit in each pepper to create a nice deep pocket for stuffing. Remove and discard the seeds and membranes from the peppers. Gently stuff each pepper with 1 to 2 tablespoons of the filling, depending on the size.

To serve, arrange the stuffed peppers on a serving dish and drizzle with the oil. Finish with a few grinds of pepper.

Georgian Eggplant Rolls

Рулети з баклажана

SERVES 4 TO 6

2 large or 4 medium Chinese eggplants, about 2 pounds total

Salt

About 1 cup sunflower oil, for frying

FOR THE FILLING

1½ cups walnut halves, toasted

½ cup tightly packed fresh cilantro leaves and cut-up stems, roughly chopped

¼ cup tightly packed fresh flat-leaf parsley leaves, roughly chopped

1 green onion, white and green parts, roughly chopped

1 garlic clove, minced

2 teaspoons red wine vinegar

½ teaspoon ground coriander

½ teaspoon ground fenugreek

¼ teaspoon ground cumin

¼ teaspoon cayenne pepper

3 tablespoons water, or more if needed

Salt and freshly ground black pepper

1 tablespoon Pomegranate Molasses (page 176), for serving

Pomegranate seeds and fresh cilantro leaves, for serving

Eggplant rolls are one of my favorite Georgian appetizers. They are the ultimate crowd-pleaser and are my first choice for taking to a vegan potluck. Make sure to sprinkle them with pomegranate seeds right before serving. And don't skip the pomegranate molasses. It really makes these rolls shine.

Line a large sheet pan with paper towels. Cut off the stem and blossom end from each eggplant. Using a mandoline or a large, sharp knife, cut each eggplant lengthwise into slices ⅛ inch thick. You should have about eight slices. Generously sprinkle the eggplant slices on both sides with salt and lay them in a single layer on the prepared pan. Let them sit for 15 minutes to draw out the excess moisture. Pat the eggplant slices completely dry with paper towels.

Line the sheet pan with fresh paper towels. In a large frying pan, heat ¼ cup of the oil over medium-high heat. Working in batches to avoid crowding, add the eggplant slices and fry, turning once, until deep brown on both sides, about 1 minute on each side. Transfer to the prepared pan to drain. Repeat with the remaining slices, adding more oil as needed. Let the slices cool to room temperature.

To make the filling, in a food processor, combine the walnuts, cilantro, parsley, green onion, garlic, vinegar, coriander, fenugreek, cumin, and cayenne and pulse until all the ingredients are finely chopped. With the processor running, start adding the water, 1 tablespoon at a time. You are aiming for a smooth, thick paste. Add more water if needed. Season the mixture to taste with salt and black pepper. (The filling can be made up to 2 days in advance and stored in an airtight container in the refrigerator. You will have more filling than you need for the rolls. Use the leftover filling in the Rustic Vegetable Salad with Walnut Dressing (page 45).

To assemble and serve the rolls, spread about 2 teaspoons of the filling on each eggplant slice, roll up the slices, and arrange the rolls, seam side down, on a serving platter. Drizzle the rolls with the pomegranate molasses and top with the pomegranate seeds and cilantro. Any leftover rolls will keep in an airtight container in the refrigerator for up to 5 days.

Panfried Zucchini

with Light Sour Cream, Herbs, and Crispy Shallot

Смажені цукіні зі сметаною

4 medium-to-small zucchini

Salt and freshly ground
black pepper

¾ cup sunflower oil

2 garlic cloves, unpeeled

2 fresh thyme sprigs

1 large shallot, halved lengthwise,
then cut into thin half-moons

¾ cup light sour cream or plain
full-fat Greek yogurt

2 tablespoons water

Small handful of fresh mint
and basil leaves

Crispy zucchini topped with garlicky sour cream has always been my favorite side dish for everything cooked on the grill. It reminds me of the early spring days when my mom and I would get the first tiny zucchini from the *bazaar*, fry them, and pack them for the trip to our annual family outing where we would feast on *shashlik* (Eastern European–style grilled meat). It would always be somewhere close to the water so my grandpas could fish and we kids could swim. Here in California, I can buy zucchini all year round, but until this day, this dish brings back memories of a warm spring breeze and the intoxicating scent of meat cooking over a live fire.

Line a sheet pan with paper towels. Halve the zucchini lengthwise and, using a paring knife, score the cut side in a crosshatch pattern. Arrange the zucchini, cut side up, in a single layer on the prepared pan. Sprinkle them with a generous pinch of salt and let them sit for 10 minutes to draw out the excess moisture.

Have ready a large plate lined with paper towels. In a large frying pan, heat ¼ cup of the oil over medium-high heat until hot and shimmering. Lower the heat to medium and place the zucchini, cut side down, in the pan. Fry until crispy and deep golden on the first side, about 7 minutes. Use the knife blade or a jar to crush one garlic clove. Then, using a spatula, turn the zucchini over and add the crushed garlic and the thyme to the pan. Lower the heat to medium-low and cook the zucchini until completely soft, 5 to 7 minutes. Remove the pan from the heat and transfer the zucchini to the prepared plate to blot the excess oil.

Have ready a small plate lined with a paper towel. In a small frying pan, heat the remaining ½ cup oil over medium-high heat. Add the shallot and fry, stirring occasionally, until golden and crispy, 4 to 5 minutes. Using a slotted spoon, scoop the shallot out of the oil and place on the prepared plate to blot the excess oil.

Finely mince the remaining garlic clove. In a small bowl, mix together the sour cream, minced garlic, and water. Season with salt and pepper.

To serve, arrange the zucchini on a medium serving platter and top with the sour cream dressing, crispy shallot, mint, and basil.

Beet Pickled Deviled Eggs

Мариновані яйці

FOR THE BRINE

2 cups water

½ cup plus 1 tablespoon distilled white vinegar

⅓ cup thinly sliced, peeled raw red beet

1 garlic clove

2 tablespoons sugar

2 teaspoons salt

½ teaspoon black peppercorns

8 hard-boiled eggs, peeled

¼ cup Horseradish Mayo (page 173)

1 tablespoon mustard powder

Salt and freshly ground black pepper

1-inch piece horseradish root, peeled and finely grated

1 tablespoon minced fresh chives

These pickled eggs have the most mesmerizing magenta color and piquant horseradish flavor. They will definitely bring a pop of color to any party table. When ready to serve, top the eggs with grated horseradish and minced chives for a dramatic—and delicious—presentation.

To make the brine, in a medium saucepan, combine all the ingredients and bring to a boil over medium-high heat. Lower the heat to a simmer and simmer for 5 minutes. Remove from the heat and let cool for a few minutes.

Place the eggs in a widemouthed glass jar and pour the hot brine over them to cover. Let the brine cool to room temperature, then cap tightly and refrigerate for at least 24 hours before serving. The eggs will keep in the brine for up to 3 days.

When ready to serve, cut the eggs in half lengthwise and remove the yolks. Reserve the egg whites. In a small bowl, combine the egg yolks, mayo, and mustard powder and mash with a fork until well mixed and smooth. Season to taste with salt and pepper.

Arrange the egg-white halves, hollow side up, on a work surface. Pipe or spoon the yolk mixture into the egg halves. Arrange the stuffed egg halves on a large serving platter, top with the horseradish and chives, and serve.

Cured Salmon

Слабосолоний лосось

SERVES 8

¼ cup plus 2½ tablespoons salt
(4 ounces)

¼ cup plus 2½ tablespoons sugar
(4 ounces)

1 small bunch fresh dill,
finely chopped

1 pound thick, skin-on
sashimi-grade salmon fillet

Curing food with salt and turning it into *solinnya* (cured or fermented food) is one of the most important Slavic preservation techniques. The equation is simple: food + salt (sometimes mixed with sugar) + time = fermentation. The longer you leave the food in salt, the longer the food will last. Ancient Slavs mastered this craft to ensure the food they preserved would sustain them through the long, barren winters. This salmon recipe is a wonderful example of quick curing, and it's beautiful in its simplicity. It requires just salt and sugar to balance the flavor and a bunch of dill for aroma. Maybe it's because of my Slavic roots, but I always tend to make cured salmon close to the winter months. It tastes delightful thinly sliced on top of dark rye bread or crispy *kremzlyky* (page 120).

You need to start curing the salmon at least 1 day before you plan to serve it. In a small bowl, mix together the salt, sugar, and dill. Spread half of the salt mixture on the bottom of a container just large enough to hold the salmon fillet.

Place the salmon, skin side down, in the container and cover it with the remaining salt mixture. Cover the container tightly with a lid or plastic wrap and refrigerate for at least 24 hours or for up to 48 hours but no longer, as the fish can get too salty and dry out.

To serve, scrape off the salt, then briefly rinse the fish with cold water and pat dry with a paper towel. Serve right away, or store in an airtight container in the refrigerator for up to 1 week.

Black Sea Pickled Mussels

Чорноморські мариновані мідії

SERVES 4

4 pounds mussels

⅓ cup water

1 small carrot, peeled and coarsely grated or thinly julienned

⅓ cup sunflower oil

1 shallot, finely chopped

1 garlic clove, minced

1 teaspoon whole coriander seeds, crushed into flakes with a mortar and pestle

¼ cup white wine vinegar

2 teaspoons sugar

1 teaspoon gochugaru (Korean red chile flakes), or ½ teaspoon cayenne pepper

½ teaspoon salt

½ cup loosely packed fresh cilantro leaves, roughly chopped

As someone who grew up near the Black Sea, I love cooking all types of clams, mussels, and other sea creatures. I haven't tasted anything like these pickled mussels anywhere else in Ukraine, so I consider this our southern dish. If you'll be anywhere near the seaside town of Kobleve, go to a local fish market. There you can taste a dozen more varieties of pickled mussels paired with a cold glass of amber beer.

Rinse the mussels well under cold running water, then lightly scrub them with a brush to rid them of mud and sand. Pull off and discard any beards (hair-like fibers) caught in the shells. (Although farmed mussels typically come with their beards removed, some can slip by intact.) Discard any mussels that do not close to the touch or have broken shells, as it means they are no longer alive.

Heat a large pot over medium-high heat. Add the mussels and water to the pot, cover tightly, and steam the mussels until their shells open wide, about 5 minutes. Remove the pot from the heat, then scoop out the mussels into a large bowl and let cool slightly. Discard any mussels that failed to open.

Remove the mussels from their shells, discarding the shells, and place the mussels in a medium bowl. Add the carrot.

In a small frying pan, heat the oil over medium-high heat. Add the shallot and cook, stirring occasionally, until lightly golden, 5 to 7 minutes. Add the garlic and coriander and cook, stirring, for 30 more seconds. Pour in the vinegar, add the sugar, gochugaru, and salt, and simmer until the sugar has dissolved, about 1 minute.

Remove from the heat, pour the hot mixture over the mussels and carrot, and toss to mix well. Let cool to room temperature, then add the cilantro and toss well with a spoon. Serve right away.

Boiled Crawfish

Варені раки

SERVES 4

8 quarts water

1 large bunch fresh dill

1 tablespoon dill seeds

1 bay leaf

2 teaspoons black peppercorns

½ cup salt

4 pounds live crawfish

2 large lemons, cut into wedges

When I was a teenager, I worked at my dad's beer stand. A few times a week, we served boiled local crawfish, and I was responsible for cooking them. I worked there all summer, so you can imagine how many pounds of crawfish I cooked. The recipe is simple and very Slavic: a bunch of dill and a generous handful of salt. These crawfish require nothing more than a few lemon wedges and a lot of cold beer.

In a large pot, combine the water, fresh dill, dill seeds, bay leaf, peppercorns, and salt and bring to a rolling boil over high heat.

While the water is heating, rinse the crawfish well under cold water, making sure to rid them of any mud and discarding any dead ones.

When the water is at a rolling boil, drop in the crawfish, cover the pot with a lid, and cook them over high heat until they turn bright red, 10 to 15 minutes.

Using a wire skimmer or other broad slotted utensil, fish the crawfish out of the water into a large bowl. Serve right away with the lemon wedges.

Spice-Rubbed Boiled Pork Belly

Шпондер

SERVES 6 TO 8

2 pounds pork belly, in one piece

8 cups water

7 tablespoons distilled white vinegar

⅓ cup salt (3½ ounces)

1 bay leaf

7 garlic cloves

1 tablespoon smoked paprika

1 teaspoon freshly ground black pepper

½ teaspoon ground coriander

½ teaspoon ground cumin

½ teaspoon cayenne pepper

Rye bread, for serving

Beet and Horseradish Hot Sauce (page 167), for serving

Known as *shponder*, this recipe is one of the countless variations of cured pork belly found in Ukraine. It is slightly more elaborate than the famous Ukrainian *salo*, which is simply salt-cured pork fat, but I also find it more delicate. Don't be discouraged by the strong vinegar scent at the beginning. Once the pork belly has cooled down, the vinegar will have evaporated. The addition of vinegar helps the pork belly achieve a buttery texture. I usually serve *shponder* thinly sliced on rye bread, topped with my homemade Beet and Horseradish Hot Sauce for a spicy kick.

In a medium saucepan, combine the pork belly, water, vinegar, salt, and bay leaf and bring to a boil over high heat. Turn down the heat to medium-low and simmer the pork belly until it can be easily pierced with a knife but still has a little resistance, about 40 minutes. Turn off the heat and let the pork belly cool down in the brine to room temperature.

Using a mortar and pestle, pound together the garlic, paprika, black pepper, coriander, cumin, and cayenne. Remove the pork belly from its brine and discard the brine. Pat the pork belly dry, then rub it on all sides with the spice mixture and wrap tightly in plastic wrap. Refrigerate for 24 hours before serving. It will keep refrigerated for up to a few weeks.

When ready to serve, using a sharp knife, cut the pork belly into thin slices and arrange on a plate. Serve with the rye and hot sauce.

Lightly Pickled Cabbage Salad

Салат "Весняний"

SERVES 6

1 pound white cabbage, thinly shredded

1 medium red bell pepper, halved, seeded, and thinly sliced crosswise

1 medium carrot, peeled and shredded

1 garlic clove, minced

1 cup water

¼ cup sunflower oil

¼ cup apple cider vinegar

2½ tablespoons sugar

2 teaspoons salt

This cabbage salad is part of the Soviet culinary legacy. It was crazy popular in those days and was served in every café and buffet in all the Soviet republics. Like all Slavic kids, I grew up eating it regularly. I usually make a large jar of this salad, as it keeps well, and every time I see it in the fridge, it brings me a strange sense of comfort.

In a large bowl, combine the cabbage, bell pepper, carrot, and garlic and mix well. Pack the cabbage mixture into a large, widemouthed heatproof glass jar.

In a small saucepan, combine the water, oil, vinegar, sugar, and salt and bring to a boil over medium-high heat, stirring with a whisk to dissolve the sugar and salt. Pour the hot brine over the cabbage mixture, making sure all of it is drenched, and let cool to room temperature. Cap the jar and refrigerate.

The salad will be ready to eat in a few hours. It will keep in the refrigerator for up to 1 week.

Rustic Vegetable Salad

with Walnut Dressing

Овочевий салат з волоськими горіхами

SERVES 2 TO 4

FOR THE DRESSING

⅔ cup raw walnut halves

1 garlic clove, minced

¼ cup water

2 tablespoons unrefined sunflower oil

1 tablespoon red wine vinegar

½ teaspoon ground coriander

½ teaspoon ground fenugreek

¼ teaspoon cayenne pepper

Salt and freshly ground black pepper

2 large tomatoes, cut into 1-inch-thick wedges

1 large Persian cucumber, cut into ¼-inch-thick slices

1 medium yellow or orange bell pepper, halved, seeded, and cut crosswise into ¼-inch-wide slices

1 jalapeño chile, thinly sliced

1 small red onion, halved through the stem end, then cut into thin half-moons

Salt

1 cup loosely packed mixed fresh herb leaves (such as basil, cilantro, parsley, and dill), roughly chopped or left whole

When my husband and I traveled to Georgia for my culinary research, every time we had a meal at someone's house, this salad was on the table. It goes lovely with *khachapuri*, a rich Georgian flatbread (page 113); fried potatoes; and all kinds of grilled meat.

To make the dressing, in a food processor, combine the walnuts, garlic, water, oil, vinegar, coriander, fenugreek, and cayenne and pulse until the mixture is smooth. Season to taste with salt and pepper and pulse briefly one more time to mix. The dressing should have a yogurt-like consistency. Thin with a couple of tablespoons of water if needed. Taste and adjust the seasoning with salt and black pepper and more vinegar if needed.

To assemble the salad, on a large platter, arrange the tomatoes, cucumber, bell pepper, chile, and onion. Sprinkle the vegetables with a small pinch of salt. Spoon the dressing evenly over the salad, then top with the herbs and serve.

Herby White Bean Salad

Салат з білої квасолі

2 cups dried cannellini beans, picked over and rinsed

5 cups water

1 bay leaf

2 fresh thyme sprigs

Salt and freshly ground black pepper

2 tablespoons refined sunflower oil

1 large leek, white part only, halved lengthwise, then thinly sliced crosswise

2 garlic cloves, minced

¼ cup tightly packed fresh dill fronds

¼ cup tightly packed fresh flat-leaf parsley leaves

¼ cup tightly packed fresh cilantro leaves

¼ cup tightly packed fresh mint leaves

2 tablespoons unrefined sunflower oil or extra-virgin olive oil

Grated zest and juice of 1 small lemon, or to taste

Toasted sourdough bread, for serving

This salad is quite simple and rustic. That's why it's crucial to use the best-quality beans you can find. I like using cannellini beans from Rancho Gordo, a specialty producer in Napa County. They have the loveliest texture and flavor. Cook them until soft and buttery with a pinch of salt and a bay leaf to bring in extra flavor.

Put the beans into a medium bowl, add the water, and leave to soak at room temperature for at least 6 hours or preferably overnight.

Drain the beans, transfer them to a saucepan, and add water to cover by 2 to 3 inches. Add the bay leaf, thyme, and a good pinch of salt and bring to a boil over medium-high heat. Lower the heat to a simmer and simmer the beans until they are soft but not mushy, 45 to 60 minutes.

While the beans are cooking, in a medium frying pan, heat the refined sunflower oil over medium heat. Add the leek and cook, stirring occasionally, until soft, about 12 minutes. Add the garlic and cook, stirring, for 30 more seconds, then remove the pan from the heat and set aside.

When the beans are cooked, drain them well, pick out and discard the herbs, and transfer them to a medium bowl. Let them cool for 10 minutes. Finely chop the dill, parsley, cilantro, and mint, add the herbs to the warm beans, and stir with a large spoon. Add the fried leek, unrefined sunflower oil, and lemon zest and juice and season to taste with salt and pepper. Mix well, then taste and adjust the seasoning with more lemon juice and zest, salt, and pepper if needed.

Serve the salad warm or at room temperature with slices of toasted sourdough.

Golden Beet Vinegret Salad

Вінегрет з жовтих буряків

3 medium golden beets

Salt and freshly ground
black pepper

3 medium carrots

2 large Yukon Gold potatoes

1 cup shelled green peas
(fresh or frozen)

5 large kosher dill pickles

½ cup Pickled Red Onion (page 160)

¼ cup chopped fresh dill and
flat-leaf parsley, in equal parts

⅓ cup unrefined sunflower oil

2 teaspoons red wine vinegar

¼ teaspoon sugar

This traditional Slavic beet salad is called *vinegret*. I came up with this version of the recipe when I ran out of red beets and fresh onions. I found a few golden beets and a jar of pickled red onions in my fridge, and I decided to give it a go. The salad came out so vibrant and beautiful that now I make this version more often than the traditional one. The only thing I would never change is the unrefined sunflower oil. That is what makes this salad taste authentic.

In a medium saucepan, combine the beets with water to cover by about 2 inches and a pinch of salt. Bring to a boil over medium-high heat and cook until the beets can be easily pierced with a knife, 30 to 40 minutes. In a separate medium saucepan, cook the carrots and potatoes using the same method. When the vegetables are ready, drain them, transfer them to a medium bowl, and let them cool to room temperature, about 30 minutes.

Meanwhile, bring a small saucepan filled with water to a boil. Fill a small bowl with ice-cold water. Season the boiling water with a pinch of salt, then add the peas and blanch until they are bright green and no longer taste starchy, about 2 minutes. Drain the peas and immerse them in the ice-cold water until they are completely cool, 3 to 5 minutes. Drain the peas and spread them on a paper towel to dry.

When the beets, potatoes, and carrots are room temperature, peel them, cut them into ¼-inch cubes, and transfer them to a large bowl. Cut the pickles and pickled onion into the same-size cubes and add them to the bowl along with the peas, dill, and parsley.

In a small bowl, mix together the oil, vinegar, and sugar with a fork, then season to taste with salt and pepper. Drizzle as much of the dressing as you like over the salad; you may not need all of it. Mix well with a large spoon, then taste and add more dressing and salt if needed.

Enjoy the salad at room temperature or chilled. It will keep in an airtight container in the refrigerator for up to 3 days.

Vegetarian Russian Potato Salad

Вегетаріанський салат Олів'є

SERVES 4 TO 6

4 medium Yukon Gold potatoes

2 medium carrots, peeled

Salt and freshly ground
black pepper

1 cup shelled green peas
(fresh or frozen)

½ cup mayonnaise

3 tablespoons sour cream

5 hard-boiled eggs, peeled

5 medium kosher dill pickles

¼ cup chopped fresh dill

¼ cup chopped fresh
flat-leaf parsley

3 tablespoons chopped fresh chives

You will not be able to find a more beloved Russian salad than *salat Olivier*. It was created in the 1860s by Lucien Olivier, a Belgian chef who worked in one of Moscow's most elegant restaurants, Hermitage. The salad consisted of expensive and rare ingredients, such as smoked duck, crayfish tails, and caviar, but has gone through many changes since its inception. During Soviet rule, it lost its expensive ingredients and became the beloved staple of common people. Unlike the Soviet version, which traditionally includes meat of some kind, mine is vegetarian and is packed with fresh herbs and green peas. I once tasted it prepared this way at my friend Rusi's house. Rusi is originally from Georgia, and she told me that in her family, *Olivier* is always vegetarian and calls for lots of fresh herbs and freshly ground black pepper, which completely blew my mind. I loved her salad so much that I've been making it this way ever since.

In a medium saucepan, combine the potatoes and carrots with water to cover by about 2 inches and bring to a boil over medium-high heat. Lower the heat to medium and cook until the vegetables are easily pierced with a knife, 20 to 25 minutes. Drain the vegetables and let cool to room temperature.

Meanwhile, bring a small saucepan filled with water to a boil. Fill a small bowl with ice-cold water. Season the boiling water with a pinch of salt, then add the peas and blanch until they are bright green and no longer taste starchy, about 2 minutes. Drain the peas and immerse them in the ice-cold water until they are completely cool, 3 to 5 minutes. Drain the peas and spread them on a paper towel to dry.

In a small bowl, whisk together the mayonnaise and sour cream to make a dressing.

Cut two of the eggs lengthwise into thick wedges. Peel the potatoes. Cut the potatoes, carrots, pickles, and the remaining three eggs into ¼-inch cubes. Transfer them all to a large bowl. Add the dressing, dill, parsley, and chives and mix well with a large spoon. Season to taste with salt and pepper and mix one more time.

Spoon the salad onto a large platter, garnish with the egg wedges, and serve right away. Leftover salad will keep in an airtight container in the refrigerator for up to 3 days.

Georgian Beet and Walnut Spread

Пхалі з буряка

SERVES 4

2 medium red beets,
about 1 pound total weight

1½ cups raw walnut halves

⅓ cup tightly packed fresh cilantro
leaves, plus more for serving

⅓ cup tightly packed fresh
flat-leaf parsley leaves

2 garlic cloves, minced

1 tablespoon red wine vinegar

½ teaspoon ground coriander

¼ teaspoon ground fenugreek

1 tablespoon Pomegranate Molasses
(page 176), plus more for serving

Salt and freshly ground
black pepper

2 tablespoons pomegranate seeds,
for garnish

Pkhali is a traditional Georgian walnut spread made with various vegetables or greens, walnuts, herbs, and garlic. I have tried many variations of this dish, but beet *pkhali* remains my favorite version. I love its intense flavor and gorgeous pink color. Together with eggplant rolls (page 29) and flatbread (page 113), it makes a bountiful *supra*-style dinner. I always serve *pkhali* drizzled with homemade pomegranate molasses and a generous amount of fresh pomegranate seeds.

In a medium saucepan, combine the beets with water to cover by about 2 inches. Bring to a boil over medium-high heat and cook until the beets are easily pierced with a knife, 30 to 40 minutes. Drain the beets and let them sit for about 10 minutes. When they are cool enough to handle, peel them and then finely grate them. Transfer them to a medium bowl and set aside.

In a food processor, combine the walnuts, cilantro, parsley, garlic, vinegar, coriander, and fenugreek and pulse until the walnuts and herbs are finely chopped. Add the beets and pomegranate molasses and pulse a few more times to combine. You should have a thick paste that can hold its shape.

Transfer the walnut-beet mixture to a medium bowl and season to taste with salt and pepper. Cover the bowl with plastic wrap and refrigerate for about 1 hour.

When ready to serve, shape the mixture into thick patties about 2 inches in diameter and arrange them on a serving plate. Top each patty with a few pomegranate seeds and cilantro leaves and drizzle them with pomegranate molasses.

Summer Squash Spread

Кабачкова ікра

SERVES 4

Sunflower oil, for frying

1 medium yellow onion, cut into ¼-inch dice

1 medium carrot, peeled and coarsely grated

1 garlic clove, minced

1½ tablespoons tomato paste

1 pound yellow summer squash, cut into ½-inch cubes

1 teaspoon apple cider vinegar, or more if needed

1 teaspoon sugar

Salt and freshly ground black pepper

I love this bright orange spread because it tastes like summer to me. For some unknown reason, we call it *kabachkova ikra* (squash caviar). Spoiler alert: I also have an eggplant caviar recipe in this book (page 57). Don't ask me why Slavic people like to call vegetable spreads caviar. I'm as puzzled as you are, especially because the spreads are almost always vegan, and no caviar can be found near them. But no matter what you call them, they will always taste amazing. Serve this spread with toasted bread or warm pita.

In a large, deep sauté pan, heat 2 tablespoons oil over medium heat. Add the onion and sauté until translucent, about 5 minutes. Add the carrot and continue cooking, stirring occasionally, until the vegetables are soft, about 7 minutes. Stir in the garlic and tomato paste and cook, stirring occasionally, until the garlic is fragrant, about 1 minute. Add the squash, stir well, and cook until the squash is hot. Turn down the heat to medium-low, cover, and cook, stirring from time to time, until the squash is very soft, 20 to 30 minutes.

Transfer the cooked vegetables to a blender, let cool for a minute or two, and puree until smooth. Return the puree to the pan and heat gently over low heat. Add the vinegar and sugar and stir until the sugar dissolves. Season the mixture to taste with salt and pepper and with more vinegar if needed. Remove from the heat and transfer to a medium bowl to cool.

Serve warm, at room temperature, or chilled. Leftover spread will keep in an airtight container in the refrigerator for up to 5 days.

Southern-Style Eggplant Caviar

Ікра з баклажанів

SERVES 4

2 pounds Japanese eggplants

1 large red bell pepper

¼ cup sunflower oil

1 large yellow onion, diced

2 garlic cloves, minced

12 ounces medium tomatoes, flesh finely grated on a box grater and skin discarded

½ cup chopped fresh cilantro leaves

Salt and freshly ground black pepper

note: If your tomatoes do not provide enough flavor and complexity, you can season the eggplant spread with a pinch of sugar and a splash of red wine vinegar.

Like the squash spread on page 54, this is one of the Slavic "caviars" made with Ukraine's wealth of summertime vegetables. It reminds me very much of Mediterranean eggplant spreads, but this one is made with no spices except for black pepper. The flavor comes from the perfectly ripe vegetables, fried onion, fresh cilantro, and garlic. It goes well with panfried potatoes and rye bread.

Preheat the oven to 450°F. Line a large sheet pan with aluminum foil.

Arrange the eggplants and the bell pepper in a single layer on the prepared pan and roast, turning them once or twice, until the vegetables are very soft and their skin is dark and wrinkly, about 40 minutes. Transfer the vegetables to a large bowl, cover the bowl with plastic wrap, and leave to steam and loosen the skin, about 10 minutes.

When the eggplants and pepper are cool enough to handle but still warm, using a paring knife, peel off and discard the skin. Trim off the stem end from the eggplants. Slit the pepper open and remove and discard the seeds and membranes. Using a large knife, chop the flesh of the eggplants and pepper as finely as you can and transfer them to a heatproof medium bowl. Set aside.

In a large frying pan, heat the oil over medium-high heat. Add the onion and fry, stirring occasionally, until golden brown and crispy, about 15 minutes. Add the garlic and fry, stirring, for 30 more seconds.

Remove the pan from the heat and pour the hot onion mixture with all its oil over the eggplant mixture. Add the tomatoes and cilantro and mix well with a large spoon, then season to taste with salt and pepper.

Serve warm, at room temperature, or chilled. Leftover spread will keep in an airtight container in the refrigerator for up to 5 days.

Tvorog Herby Spread

Сирна намазка

SERVES 4

8 ounces tvorog cheese, homemade (page 174) or store-bought

1 garlic clove, minced

½ cup tightly packed mixed fresh herb leaves (such as dill, mint, and flat-leaf parsley) and cut-up green onion

1 small Persian cucumber, grated and then squeezed to release excess moisture

Salt and freshly ground black pepper

This light, herby spread always reminds me of early spring, when outdoor markets in Ukraine are bursting with the season's first greens and tender, leafy herbs, crisp, young cucumbers, and slender green onions. For the most authentic experience, I highly recommend serving this spread with crunchy slices of toasted dark rye bread.

In a food processor, combine the cheese, garlic, and herbs and process until the mixture is smooth. Transfer the mixture to a small bowl, add the cucumber, and mix well with a spoon. Season to taste with salt and pepper.

Serve the spread right away, or transfer to an airtight container and refrigerate for up to 3 days.

Famous Odessa Forshmak

Одеський форшмак

SERVES 4

2 ounces crustless soft white bread (about 1½ slices), cut into 1-inch cubes

⅓ cup heavy cream

8 ounces skinless herring fillet, roughly chopped

1 hard-boiled egg, peeled and chopped

1 small green apple, peeled, halved, cored, and cubed

4 tablespoons cold unsalted butter, cubed

3 tablespoons minced shallot

¼ teaspoon white pepper

Apple cider vinegar, for seasoning

Salt

1 ounce salmon roe (about 2 tablespoons), optional

2 tablespoons thinly sliced green onion, green part only

Toasted rye bread, for serving

 note: If you feel comfortable filleting a whole herring, I recommend you buy whole Haifa brand herrings from a Slavic store. Otherwise, look for Santa Bremor "matjes" herring fillets in oil. There are usually plenty of different options in the refrigerated section in Slavic stores, but I like the one labeled "Original" the best.

Forshmak, which is basically herring mousse, might seem like an odd dish to some people, but I assure you it's worth trying. The first time I tasted it was in a Jewish restaurant in Odessa, and it was an instant hit with me. When I moved to San Francisco, I added *forshmak* to my Odessa-inspired pop-up dinner menu, and people loved it. When a lady from Odessa told me that my version was the best one she had ever tasted, I knew I was doing something right in this life.

Put the bread cubes into a small bowl, pour in the cream, and let the bread soak for about 20 minutes.

Squeeze the bread with your hands to remove as much liquid as possible, then put the bread into a food processor. Add the herring, egg, apple, butter, shallot, and pepper to the processor and process until a smooth paste forms. Taste, add a splash of the vinegar, and then season with a pinch of salt if needed and mix well.

Spoon the paste onto a small serving plate and top with the salmon roe, if using, and the green onion. Serve with the rye.

SOUPS AND KASHAS

✤ ✤ ✤

✤ ✤ ✤

СУПИ І КАШІ

SINCE ANCIENT TIMES, soup and kasha (grain porridge) have been central to everyday Eastern European cooking. Historically, the region's climate and soil were perfect for growing all types of grains and pseudocereals, such as wheat, barley, rye, millet, and buckwheat. Because potatoes and corn, two of Ukraine's largest crops and most important kitchen staples, did not arrive in the country until the seventeenth century, grains were used to create all kinds of hearty soups and kashas to nourish and comfort people after long days of hard physical work. Today these dishes are usually served between the *zakusky* and the main dishes.

Eastern European cuisine boasts a nearly endless list of soups. They are typically based on broth made with meat or fish and can be enriched with pasta, simple dumplings such as *galushky*, or a generous handful of grains or legumes. One of the most iconic Slavic soups, which is famous far beyond Eastern Europe, is borscht. There are three main types of borscht: red borscht, which is made with beets, cabbage, and other vegetables; green or spring borscht, which combines such luscious greens as sorrel, spinach, stinging nettles, and beet tops; and cold summer borscht, made with crispy radishes, cucumbers, and a splash of tangy kefir. All three types are unique and special, and since they are an essential part of my culinary heritage, I have included them all in this book.

The types of kasha eaten vary from region to region and country to country. Western Ukraine, Romania, and Moldova lean toward *banosh*, a creamy cornmeal-based kasha. Other areas, such as southern and eastern Ukraine, Russia, and Belarus, tend to favor buckwheat- and barley-based kashas. Savory kasha is usually served with fried onion, mushrooms, and all kinds of stewed or fried meats. Sweet kasha is typically cooked with pumpkin, butternut squash, or various orchard fruits and berries. To honor this tradition, I have showcased two of my favorite kasha recipes in this chapter, one sweet and one savory.

Cold Borscht

Холодник

SERVES 6

2 medium red beets, about
12 ounces total weight

5 hard-boiled eggs, peeled

3 cups plain kefir or buttermilk

2 medium Persian cucumbers,
thinly sliced

3 medium radishes, thinly sliced

¼ cup finely chopped fresh dill and
flat-leaf parsley, in equal parts, plus
more for serving

Distilled water, chilled, if needed
for thinning

Salt and freshly ground
black pepper

2 green onions, green part only,
thinly sliced

½ cup full-fat plain Greek yogurt

Extra-virgin olive oil, for serving

Ukrainians call this cold borscht *kholodnyk* (*kholod* means "cold" in both Ukrainian and Russian). It is incredibly refreshing, and we eat it during the blazing-hot Ukrainian days of summer. When the weather is simply unbearable, eating a bowl of this soup makes you feel invigorated again. I always use a lot of fresh, crisp vegetables and flavorful herbs to add more texture and to introduce even more vibrant colors.

In a medium saucepan, combine the beets with water to cover by about 2 inches. Bring to a boil over medium-high heat and cook until the beets are easily pierced with a knife, 30 to 40 minutes. Drain the beets and let them sit for about 10 minutes. When they are cool enough to handle, peel them and then coarsely grate them. Return them to the pot.

Coarsely grate two of the eggs and add them to the beets. Add the kefir, about half each of the cucumbers and radishes (reserve the remainder for finishing the soup), and the dill and parsley. Mix together everything with a spoon and then add a bit of the chilled water if the mixture is too thick. It should be the consistency of a yogurt soup. Season to taste with salt and pepper. Cover the pot and chill for at least 30 minutes or for up to 2 hours before serving.

When ready to serve, halve the remaining three eggs lengthwise. Ladle the soup into bowls. Top each serving with some of the remaining cucumbers and radishes, the green onions, egg halves, a dollop of yogurt, some dill and parsley, and a generous drizzle of oil. The soup needs to be eaten very cold, right from the fridge. It tastes best the day it is made.

Vegetarian Borscht

with Chanterelle Mushrooms and Prunes

Вегетаріанський борщ з лисичками і чорносливом

SERVES 6

3 tablespoons unsalted butter

1 tablespoon sunflower oil

1 medium yellow onion, finely chopped

2 medium carrots, peeled and shredded

1 medium tomato, diced

4 medium Yukon Gold potatoes, peeled and cut into 1½-inch cubes

2 medium red beets, peeled and cut into matchsticks

1 small bell pepper, seeded and thinly sliced

1½ cups chanterelle mushrooms, halved lengthwise

4 prunes, pitted and roughly chopped

2 bay leaves

Salt and freshly ground black pepper

½ cup drained canned white beans, rinsed

1 small head green cabbage, cored and shredded

2 garlic cloves, minced

¼ cup chopped fresh dill and flat-leaf parsley, in equal parts

Sour cream, for serving

Pampushky (page 116), for serving

Sour cream and dill on everything is our family motto. Just kidding, as there's also garlic. And this flavorful vegetarian mushroom borscht is no exception. I added some beautiful prunes for sweetness and chanterelle mushrooms for a deep, earthy taste. It's a very traditional flavor combination that is rarely used today. We take our borscht very seriously in Ukraine. At some point, it may even become illegal to eat it without sour cream. I know that I've never seen a bowl that did not include a finishing dollop. In fact, the thought of eating borscht without rich sour cream on top and garlicky *pampushky* on the side makes me cringe. I guess that makes me a true borscht patriot.

In a medium-large pot, melt the butter with the oil over medium heat. Add the onion and carrots and cook, stirring occasionally, until soft, 7 to 9 minutes. Add the tomato and cook, stirring from time to time, for 2 minutes longer.

Now it's time to add water (or vegetable broth, if you prefer). It is always a bit tricky to say how much because the ideal amount is never the same. It will depend on how big your pot is and the volume of your vegetables. For me, it's usually 3 to 3½ quarts, but I never measure the exact amount. You want enough to cover all the vegetables by about 1 inch. You can always add more water later if needed. Once the water is in the pot, add the potatoes, beets, bell pepper, mushrooms, prunes, and bay leaves and bring the mixture to a boil over medium-high heat. Add a generous pinch of salt, turn down the heat to medium-low, and simmer, uncovered, until the potatoes are soft when pierced with a knife, about 15 minutes.

Add the beans and cabbage and cook, stirring occasionally, until all the vegetables are soft, 10 to 15 minutes. Add the garlic, dill, and parsley and season to taste with salt and pepper. Stir to combine and cook for 2 more minutes. Remove and discard the bay leaves.

Ladle the borscht into bowls and top each serving with a dollop of sour cream. Serve right away with the pampushky on the side.

Green Sorrel Borscht

with Semisoft Egg

Зелений борщ

SERVES 6

1 pound bone-in,
skin-on chicken thighs

2 large yellow onions

1 bay leaf

Salt and black pepper

8 cups water

12 ounces Yukon Gold potatoes,
peeled and cut into ¾-inch cubes

2 tablespoons unsalted butter

1 tablespoon sunflower oil

2 medium carrots, peeled and
shredded

⅓ cup heavy cream

6 ounces baby spinach,
roughly chopped

3 ounces sorrel, roughly chopped

2 hard-boiled eggs, peeled and
chopped into ½-inch pieces

¼ cup chopped fresh dill and
flat-leaf parsley, in equal parts

¼ cup sour cream, for serving

3 semisoft-boiled eggs, peeled and
halved (see Note)

note: To cook the semisoft-
boiled eggs, bring a medium
saucepan filled with water to a
boil. Meanwhile, fill a bowl with
ice-cold water. Lower the eggs
into the boiling water, and cook for
6½ minutes. Scoop out the eggs
and immerse them in the ice-cold
water. Then peel them and cut in
half lengthwise.

Despite the common perception, not all borscht is red. In this book, you'll find three borscht recipes, one is neon pink and served cold for hot summer weather, one is hearty and reddish purple for chilly winter days, and this one is green with chopped eggs for the lovely springtime. My mother-in-law makes a wonderful green borscht with a mixture of deep green, vegetal spinach and zesty sorrel. In my version of her dish, I add halved semisoft eggs to make it even more photogenic.

In a medium-large pot, combine the chicken thighs, one of the whole onions, the bay leaf, 1 teaspoon salt, and the water and bring to a simmer over medium-high heat. Lower the heat to medium-low and cook uncovered, skimming off any foam and impurities from the surface as they develop, until the chicken is cooked through, about 30 minutes.

Remove the chicken and onion from the pot. When the chicken is cool enough to handle, slice the meat off the bones, remove the skin, and cut the meat into bite-size pieces. Discard the skin, bones, and the whole onion and return the meat to the pot. Add the potatoes, bring to a simmer over medium heat, and cook until the potatoes are easily pierced with a knife, about 15 minutes.

Meanwhile, finely dice the remaining onion. In a medium sauté pan, melt the butter with the oil over medium heat. Add the onion and carrots and cook, stirring occasionally, until the onion is soft and translucent, about 7 minutes.

Transfer the onion-carrot mixture to the soup and simmer for about 3 minutes to blend the flavors. Stir in the cream, spinach, and sorrel, bring to a simmer, and cook until the greens are wilted, about 2 minutes. Add the chopped eggs, season to taste with salt and pepper, and remove from the heat. Remove and discard the bay leaf.

Ladle the soup into bowls. Garnish each serving with some of the dill and parsley, a dollop of sour cream, and an egg half and serve right away.

Buckwheat Soup

with Wild Mushrooms

Гречаний суп з грибами

SERVES 8

½ ounce dried wild mushrooms (about ⅓ cup)

1 tablespoon unsalted butter

1 tablespoon sunflower oil

1 medium yellow onion, finely diced

1 small carrot, peeled and shredded

2½ quarts vegetable broth

4 medium Yukon Gold potatoes, peeled and cut into 1½-inch cubes

6 ounces mixed fresh mushrooms (such as cremini, shiitake, and chanterelle), thinly sliced

¼ cup toasted buckwheat, rinsed and drained

1 bay leaf

Salt and freshly ground black pepper

2 tablespoons chopped fresh flat-leaf parsley, for serving

Sour cream, for serving

Buckwheat is the most popular grain in Slavic cuisine. When a crisis hits any Slavic country, buckwheat is usually the first thing that disappears from grocery store shelves. That's how much people rely on it in their diet. I was never crazy about buckwheat when I was a kid. But when mom made me this soup, everything changed. It has the most alluring deep flavor of buckwheat and mushrooms with the right balance of sweetness and earthiness. It's just like being wrapped in a cozy blanket and taking an autumn walk in a forest. I love eating this soup piping hot with the darkest rye bread I can find.

Put the dried mushrooms into a small heatproof bowl and pour in boiling water to cover. Let the mushrooms rehydrate for at least 20 minutes. Drain the mushrooms through a fine-mesh sieve placed over a small bowl. Roughly slice the mushrooms. Set the mushrooms and reserved liquid aside separately.

In a large frying pan, melt the butter with the oil over medium-high heat. Add the onion and cook, stirring often, until translucent, about 7 minutes. Add the carrot and continue cooking, stirring often, until the vegetables are soft, 7 to 10 minutes longer. Remove the pan from the heat.

In a medium pot, combine the broth, mushroom water, potatoes, and rehydrated mushrooms and bring to a boil over high heat. Lower the heat to medium and cook for about 10 minutes. Add the onion-carrot mixture and the fresh mushrooms, raise the heat to medium-high, and bring to a boil. Add the buckwheat and bay leaf and season with salt and pepper. Lower the heat to medium and simmer until the buckwheat is tender, about 15 minutes. Remove from the heat and remove and discard the bay leaf.

Ladle the soup into deep bowls. Top each serving with parsley and a dollop of sour cream and serve right away.

Chicken Soup

with Hand-Cut Noodles

Курячий суп з яєчною лапшою

SERVES 8

FOR THE NOODLES

2¼ cups all-purpose flour, plus more if needed and for dusting

3 whole eggs

2 egg yolks

1 tablespoon sunflower oil

1 teaspoon salt

1 tablespoon semolina

FOR THE SOUP

1 whole chicken, 3 to 3½ pounds

4 large celery stalks

2 medium carrots, peeled

1 medium yellow onion

4 fresh flat-leaf parsley sprigs

1 fresh thyme sprig

1 bay leaf

½ teaspoon black peppercorns

Salt and freshly ground black pepper

12 ounces small new potatoes

1 medium parsnip, peeled and halved lengthwise

1 medium bell pepper, halved and seeded

Lyok (page 167), for serving

Despite the lack of scientific proof, chicken soup is considered the remedy for almost any illness in Ukraine. Every time I had a cold, upset stomach, or a headache, my grandma would cook chicken soup for me. Usually she made a simple and hearty chicken broth and flavored it with a bunch of fresh dill, but on special occasions, she would add her homemade egg noodles and serve a small bowl of herby-garlicky *lyok* on the side. To this day, her chicken noodle soup is my go-to remedy whenever I feel under the weather.

To make the noodles, sift the flour onto a clean work surface. Make a well in the center and add the whole eggs, egg yolks, oil, and salt to the well. Carefully whisk the egg mixture with a fork until combined. Start gently scooping small portions of the flour into the well and incorporating them into the egg mixture. When all the flour has been mixed with the egg mixture and the dough comes together into a shaggy mass, start kneading the dough with your hands. Continue kneading until the dough is fairly smooth, about 5 minutes. If the dough feels too sticky, knead in a little more flour. Tightly wrap the dough in plastic wrap and let it rest at room temperature for 30 minutes.

You'll notice that the dough will have become much smoother during resting. Clean the work surface, then dust it lightly with flour. Unwrap the dough and divide it into four equal portions. One at a time, roll out each portion as thinly as possible into a large rectangle. Aim for the thickness of fettuccine. Let the dough sheets air-dry for 5 to 10 minutes.

Lightly dust a large sheet pan with the semolina. Lightly sprinkle the dough sheets with flour and loosely roll up each sheet into a tube. Gently flatten each tube with your palm. Using a large, sharp knife, cut across each tube to make ¼-inch-wide noodles. Unroll the noodles and spread them on the prepared pan. Leave to dry for at least 20 minutes or for up to a few hours before cooking.

To make the soup, place the chicken in a large pot. Roughly chop two of the celery stalks and one of the carrots and add them to the pot along with the whole onion, parsley, thyme, bay leaf, and peppercorns. Add just enough water to barely cover the chicken and bring to a boil over medium-high heat. Lower the heat to medium-low and simmer, skimming off any foam and impurities from the surface as they develop, until the chicken is fully cooked (no longer pink when you cut close to the thigh bone), about 45 minutes.

Remove the chicken from the broth, place it on a platter, and cover with plastic wrap. Set aside until ready to serve. Strain the broth and return it to the pot.

Return the broth to the stove top and season it with a pinch of salt. Then drop in the potatoes and bring the broth to a boil over medium-high heat. Turn down the heat to medium-low and cook the potatoes for about 10 minutes.

Meanwhile, cut the remaining two celery stalks, one carrot, the parsnip, and the bell pepper into ¼-inch-thick half-moons and drop them into the soup. Continue simmering until the potatoes and other vegetables are soft when pierced with a knife, about 15 minutes. Taste the broth and season with more salt if needed. Raise the heat to medium-high and bring the soup to a boil. Drop in the noodles and continue cooking the soup for 3 more minutes. Remove the pot from the heat and remove and discard the bay leaf.

Carve the chicken into eight serving pieces and place them in wide soup bowls. Ladle the hot noodle soup over the chicken and top each serving with a generous dollop of lyok and a couple of grinds of pepper.

Soup with Buckwheat Dumplings

Суп з гречаними галушками

SERVES 6

FOR THE SOUP

½ large chicken, 1¾ to 2 pounds

2½ to 3 quarts water

1 tablespoon sunflower oil

1 medium yellow onion, diced

1 medium carrot, peeled and shredded

¾ cup diced tomatoes (fresh or canned)

2 teaspoons tomato paste

¼ cup heavy cream

3 medium Yukon Gold potatoes, cut into 1-inch pieces

1 bay leaf

¼ teaspoon black peppercorns

Salt

3 celery stalks, cut into ¼-inch-thick half-moons

1 medium red bell pepper, quartered, seeded, and thinly sliced crosswise

FOR THE DUMPLINGS

1 egg

¼ cup club soda

¼ teaspoon salt

¼ cup plus 1 tablespoon all-purpose flour

2 tablespoons buckwheat flour

Soul-warming soups are integral to Slavic cuisine. This one is especially close to my heart because it includes a bunch of airy dumplings, or *galushky*, floating on top. *Galushky* are usually made with all-purpose flour, but I decided to mix in a handful of buckwheat flour. I love how it deepens the flavor and adds complexity to the dumplings.

Place the chicken half in a medium-large pot and pour in the water as needed to cover. Bring to a boil over medium-high heat, then lower the heat to medium-low and simmer, skimming off any foam and impurities from the surface as they develop, until the chicken is fully cooked (no longer pink when you cut close to the thigh bone), about 40 minutes.

Meanwhile, in a large sauté pan, heat the oil over medium heat. Add the onion and cook, stirring occasionally, until translucent, about 5 minutes. Add the carrot and cook, stirring occasionally, until both vegetables are soft, 7 to 10 minutes. Add the tomatoes and tomato paste and simmer, until tomatoes are soft and mushy, about 5 minutes. Stir in the cream and remove from the heat.

When the chicken is ready, remove it from the broth and place it on a large cutting board to cool.

Add the tomato mixture to the broth, followed by the potatoes, bay leaf, peppercorns, and a pinch of salt. Bring to a simmer over medium heat and cook until the potatoes begin to soften, about 10 minutes. Add the celery and bell pepper and continue to simmer until all the vegetables are soft, 10 to 15 minutes. Remove and discard the bay leaf.

Meanwhile, pick the meat off the chicken carcass and tear it into bite-size pieces, discarding the skin and bones.

To make the dumplings, in a small bowl, combine the egg, club soda, and salt and whisk together with a fork until well mixed. Then add both flours and whisk until a batter forms. It should have the consistency of yogurt.

Return the chicken meat to the soup. Raise the heat to medium-high and bring the soup to an active boil. Dip a teaspoon into the hot soup, scoop up a little batter with the hot spoon, and drop the batter into the simmering soup. Dipping the spoon into the hot soup helps the batter glide off the spoon without sticking. Repeat, dipping the spoon into the hot soup before forming each dumpling, until all of the batter has been used. The batter portions should be no larger than uncooked gnocchi because the dumplings will be double in size when they are fully cooked. Lower the heat to medium and let the soup simmer until the dumplings are floating on top, about 5 minutes, then remove from the heat.

Ladle the soup and dumplings into bowls and serve right away.

Hutsul Polenta

Баныш

SERVES 4 TO 6

1 cup medium-grind grits

4 cups whole milk

1 garlic clove, minced

Salt

3 tablespoons sour cream

2 tablespoons unsalted butter

½ teaspoon ground white pepper

1 cup crumbled *bryndza* or sheep's milk feta cheese

This dish is my interpretation of traditional Ukrainian and Romanian cornmeal kasha (*banosh*), which is very similar to Italian polenta. It is a traditional dish of the Hutsuls, a small ethnic group native to the Carpathian Mountains of both Ukraine and Romania, where they have long bred sheep and cattle. The main difference between *banosh* and polenta is that *banosh* calls for a generous dollop of sour cream for extra richness. Also, instead of aged Parmigiano-Reggiano, we add *bryndza*, a young sheep's milk cheese. *Bryndza* is carried in many Russian stores, but if you cannot find it, Bulgarian or Greek feta will work equally well.

Put the grits into a fine-mesh sieve and rinse under cold running water until the water runs clear.

In a medium saucepan, bring the milk to a simmer over medium-high heat. Add the garlic, a pinch of salt, and the grits and quickly stir the mixture with a whisk to prevent it from clumping. Lower the heat to medium-low and simmer the grits, stirring frequently, until the mixture thickens and pulls away from the sides of the pan, about 40 minutes.

Stir in the sour cream, butter, and pepper and remove from the heat. Banosh must be served immediately. Pour it into a large, shallow bowl, top with the cheese or your favorite meat stew, and invite your guests to help themselves.

Sweet Pumpkin Rice Kasha

Гарбузова каша

SERVES 2

2 cups cubed, peeled pumpkin or butternut squash, in ½-inch cubes

2 tablespoons golden raisins

2 cups water

½ cup medium-grain white rice (such as Bomba or Calrose)

1⅓ cups whole milk

2 tablespoons sugar

1 teaspoon pure vanilla extract

½ teaspoon salt

1 tablespoon unsalted butter

¼ cup chopped roasted hazelnuts, for serving (optional)

This pumpkin kasha is a childhood favorite for both my husband and me. It has a lovely creamy texture and a nostalgic aroma of pumpkin and vanilla. Even though I know it's totally nontraditional, I like to sprinkle a handful of toasted hazelnuts on top to add a bit of texture.

In a medium saucepan, combine the pumpkin, raisins, and water and bring to a boil over medium-high heat. Lower the heat to medium-low, cover, and simmer until the pumpkin is soft when pierced with a knife, 10 to 15 minutes.

Meanwhile, put the rice into a fine-mesh sieve and rinse under cold running water until the water runs clear. When the pumpkin is soft, add the rice, milk, sugar, vanilla, and salt, stir well, and bring to a simmer. Turn down the heat to low and cook, stirring occasionally, until the rice is tender, 15 to 20 minutes.

Remove from the heat and stir in the butter. Ladle the kasha into bowls and top with the hazelnuts, if desired. Serve right away.

MAIN DISHES
ОСНОВНІ СТРАВИ

TRADITIONALLY, EASTERN EUROPEAN main courses tend to be rich and filling. Among the most typical dishes are cabbage rolls, stuffed bell peppers, meat and vegetable stews, pickled herring with boiled potatoes, and all kinds of fried and roasted fish. Historically, pork and chicken are the most popular meats. That's because, unlike cows and sheep, pigs and chickens grow quickly and they don't produce milk that can be used to make our favorite dairy products, such as *syr* (tangy fresh cheese) and *smetana* (sour cream). When I picked recipes for this chapter, I sought to include some simple everyday dishes you can make for a family dinner. But I also wanted to slip in a few showstoppers that you can cook to wow dinner guests.

When it comes to special occasions, the bird—typically chicken or duck—is often cooked whole and then carved right at the table. The best cuts, such as legs and breasts, are served to guests, and the least desirable parts, like the neck and bishop's nose, usually go to the hostess, which is terribly unfair in my opinion. Whole roasted duck is my grandma's specialty, and I feel this book would be incomplete without her recipe. She roasts the duck on a bed of sliced sour apples, which makes it juicy and incredibly flavorful, as you'll discover when you make it.

The main dish usually comes after the *zakusky* and soup, and it is at this point that people in my family start offering their guests a glass of their homemade wine. During my last visit to Ukraine, my grandma poured me a glass of her "light" rosé to go with the duck, and a few sips knocked me out of my socks. I forgot how strong Slavic homemade wine is. I think that even vodka hits lighter than that wine hit me, so be careful when you're drinking at people's homes—and don't say I didn't warn you.

Cabbage Rolls

with Barley and Mushrooms

Голубці з ячменем і грибами

SERVES 4 TO 6

FOR THE CABBAGE ROLLS

12 medium-size jarred pickled cabbage leaves (see Note)

2/3 cup pearl barley

1 1/3 cups vegetable broth or water

Salt and freshly ground black pepper

2 tablespoons sunflower oil

1 medium yellow onion, diced

8 ounces mushrooms (shiitake, cremini, trumpet, or chanterelle works great), sliced

FOR THE SAUCE

2 tablespoons sunflower oil

1 large yellow onion, quartered through the stem end, then thinly sliced crosswise

1 teaspoon sugar

1/4 cup water

1 cup heavy cream

2/3 cup vegetable broth or water

1 bay leaf

Salt and freshly ground black pepper

2 tablespoons chopped fresh flat-leaf parsley, for serving

Sour cream, for serving

Hearty cabbage rolls, known as *golubzi*, are a well-known Slavic staple. But this recipe is different from the classic version. First of all, it's vegetarian. Second, I use pickled cabbage leaves instead of fresh ones. They add a pleasant sourness and complexity I really enjoy. And last but not least, I have swapped the usual tomato sauce for a rich, creamy one, which brings the dish to a whole new level of comfort food. Despite the sauce already being extra creamy, I always serve this dish with a dollop of sour cream.

To make the rolls, remove the pickled cabbage leaves from the jar. Unroll them and place them in a medium-large bowl. Cover the leaves with cold water and let soak for 30 to 60 minutes. This step will make them less salty and less sour.

In a small saucepan, combine the barley, broth, and a pinch of salt and bring to a simmer over high heat. Cover, lower the heat to medium-low, and cook the barley until tender but still slightly chewy, 20 to 25 minutes. Drain the barley and set aside until needed.

Meanwhile, in a medium frying pan, heat the oil over medium heat. Add the onion and cook, stirring occasionally, until translucent and soft, 5 to 7 minutes. Add the mushrooms and cook, stirring frequently, until the mushrooms are soft and fragrant, 10 to 15 minutes. Add the barley, mix well with a spoon, and season to taste with salt and pepper. Remove from the heat and let the mixture cool to room temperature.

To make the sauce, in a large, deep ovenproof frying pan or sauté pan, heat the oil over medium heat. Add the onion and cook, stirring occasionally, until translucent, about 10 minutes. Add the sugar and mix well, then pour in the water, cover, lower the heat to medium-low, and cook, stirring occasionally, until the onion is golden and caramelized, 15 to 20 minutes. Pour in the cream and broth, add the bay leaf, raise the heat to medium-high, and bring the sauce to a simmer. Season to taste with salt and pepper and remove the pan from the heat.

Preheat the oven to 425°F.

Remove the cabbage leaves from the water and pat them dry with paper towels. If a cabbage leaf has a hard, thick rib near the base, cut it away with a paring knife, being careful not to cut too far into the leaf. Lay the cabbage leaves flat in a single layer on a work surface. To fill and shape each roll, spoon about 3 tablespoons of the filling onto a leaf, placing it toward the base. Fold in the sides and then roll up the leaf from the base, enclosing the filling.

Arrange the cabbage rolls, seam side down, in the pan with the sauce. Spoon some of the sauce over the tops of the rolls. Transfer the pan to the oven and bake, uncovered, until the sauce has thickened and the cabbage rolls are soft and golden brown, about 30 minutes.

Arrange the rolls on a serving platter and spoon the sauce over the top, discarding the bay leaf. Garnish with the parsley and serve right away, with a bowl of sour cream on the side.

note: You can buy jarred pickled cabbage leaves at almost any Slavic grocery store.

Roasted Whole Cabbage

Запечена капуста

SERVES 6

1 small head white cabbage, about 2 pounds

½ cup salted butter, at room temperature

1 teaspoon ground caraway seeds

Salt and freshly ground black pepper

1 tablespoon dill

Flaky sea salt, for finishing

Sour cream, for serving

Cabbage plays an important role in Slavic cuisine. We eat cabbage raw, we ferment and pickle it, and we shred it into soups and stews. But we never roast it whole, which is a shame. This whole roasted cabbage is a real showstopper. It looks like a golden brown savory cabbage cake. Chef Kirsten Goldberg made it one day for her students at the San Francisco Cooking School, and we were all blown away by its appearance. The minute I tasted it, I knew the recipe should be in this book because it has a very strong Slavic flavor profile. It makes a beautiful vegetarian main course served with hearty kasha on the side. But it is also lovely paired with rich meat roasts and bean stews, letting all those bold flavors step in while it still holds its own.

Preheat the oven to 300°F.

Remove the loose outer leaves of the cabbage and reserve for another use. Trim the bottom if needed so the cabbage will stand upright.

In a small bowl, combine the butter and caraway and mix well. Rub the butter mixture evenly over the entire outside of the cabbage. Stand the cabbage upright in a medium-large Dutch oven. Pour water into the bottom of the pot to come one-third of the way up the sides of the cabbage. Stir 2 teaspoons salt into the water.

Cover the pot with a round piece of parchment paper and then its lid. Place the pot on the stove and bring to a boil over medium-high heat. Transfer the pot to the oven and roast the cabbage until it is completely tender all the way through when pierced with a long, sharp knife or cake tester, about 2½ hours. Check it from time to time and add more water if needed to maintain the original level.

Remove the lid and the parchment and raise the oven temperature to 400°F. Continue to roast the cabbage until the top leaves are deep golden brown, about 15 minutes.

Transfer the cabbage to a deep serving dish and cut it into wedges. Drizzle the wedges with the pot sauce, top with flaky salt and a few grinds of pepper, and serve right away. Pass a bowl of sour cream at the table.

Herring with Pickled Onion and New Potatoes

Оселедець з молодою картоплею

SERVES 4

FOR THE POTATOES

1½ pounds small new potatoes

Salt and freshly ground
black pepper

¼ cup sour cream

1 tablespoon unsalted butter

2 garlic cloves, minced

¼ cup finely chopped fresh dill and
flat-leaf parsley, in equal parts

FOR THE HERRING

4 herring fillets (see Note, page 61)

2 tablespoons unrefined
sunflower oil

⅓ cup Pickled Red Onion (page 160)

Pickled herring and boiled potatoes are an iconic Slavic combo. If you haven't tried it yet, you are in for a treat. A lot of people don't add sour cream to their boiled potatoes, but I always do. It adds extra creaminess and makes the potatoes even more irresistible. Also, whenever you shop for a whole herring, always go for a fatty one, as it will be much more delicious. And make sure you have some vodka in the freezer, because this dish is sure to put you in the mood for an ice-cold vodka shot.

In a medium saucepan, combine the potatoes with water to cover by 2 inches and a good pinch of salt and bring to a boil over medium-high heat. Lower the heat to medium and cook until the potatoes are easily pierced with a knife, about 20 minutes.

Drain off all the water from the pan, then add the sour cream, butter, garlic, dill, parsley, and a few grinds of pepper to the potatoes. Cover the pot with a lid and shake the pot well to toss the potatoes with the sour cream and all the other delicious ingredients. Set the covered pot aside.

To prepare the herring, slice the herring fillets into 1-inch-wide pieces and arrange them attractively on a serving dish. Drizzle with the oil and top with the pickled onion.

Serve the herring immediately with the warm potatoes.

Lavash-Wrapped Halibut

with Beet Yogurt

Палтус в лаваші з буряковим йогуртом

FOR THE FISH

4 tablespoons unsalted butter, melted

2 garlic cloves, minced

1 tablespoon sweet paprika

Salt and freshly ground black pepper

4 skinless halibut fillets, 6 ounces each

4 lavash wraps, each 8 by 10 inches

4 fresh tarragon sprigs

4 fresh dill fronds

8 green onions, trimmed

1 tablespoon sunflower oil

FOR THE YOGURT

1 medium red beet, cooked, peeled, and finely diced

2 tablespoons sunflower oil

1 teaspoon red wine vinegar

1 garlic clove, minced

Salt and freshly ground black pepper

1½ cups plain full-fat Greek yogurt

Fish wrapped in thin lavash and then baked until the lavash is crisp and golden is a simple and delicious way to make a wonderful dinner in just half an hour. The inspiration for this recipe came from *Lavash*, an extraordinary Armenian cookbook written by Kate Leahy and Ara Zada. The fish comes out super flaky and delicate. I love serving it with roasted green onions and vibrant beet yogurt for a splash of color and zestiness.

Preheat the oven to 400°F. Line a sheet pan with parchment paper.

To prepare the fish, in a small bowl, mix together the butter, garlic, paprika, and a good pinch of salt. Brush both sides of each halibut fillet with the garlic butter and top with a few grinds of black pepper. Lay the lavash wraps on a work surface. Place a fillet in the center of a lavash wrap. Top the fillet with one tarragon sprig and one dill frond. Fold up the bottom of the lavash to cover the fillet, then fold in the sides and fold down the top, creating an envelope-like packet. Place the packet seam side down on the prepared pan. Repeat with the remaining lavash wraps, fish fillets, and herbs and add to the pan.

Arrange the green onions on the same pan, brush them with the oil, and sprinkle with a pinch of salt. Transfer the pan to the oven and bake until the lavash is golden and crispy and the green onions are soft and bright green, 12 to 15 minutes.

Meanwhile, make the beet yogurt. In a small bowl, toss the beet with the oil, vinegar, and garlic. Season to taste with salt and pepper, then taste and add more vinegar if needed. Put the yogurt into a small serving bowl and top with the beet mixture.

Divide the fish packets and green onions among four dinner plates and serve right away. Pass the beet yogurt at the table.

Garlicky Georgian Chicken

Курка в молоці

SERVES 4 TO 6

1 whole chicken, about 3½ pounds

2 teaspoons salt

1 teaspoon freshly ground
black pepper

½ teaspoon ground cumin

½ teaspoon ground coriander

½ teaspoon ground fenugreek

½ teaspoon dried basil

6 cups whole milk

1 head garlic, top sliced off

1 bay leaf

1 lemon zest strip, 4 to 5 inches long

Lyok (page 167), for serving

Shkmeruli, a traditional Georgian chicken dish in which chicken pieces are browned and then cooked in a garlicky milk sauce, inspired this recipe. But instead of cutting the bird into pieces, I roast it whole until the skin is golden brown and the meat falls off the bone. You can carve the chicken in the kitchen and arrange it on a platter or, for a more dramatic presentation, carve it at at the table. This chicken will have lots of delicious sauce, so be sure to serve plenty of fluffy bread to sop it up.

Pat the chicken dry with a paper towel. In a small bowl, mix together the salt, pepper, cumin, coriander, fenugreek, and basil. Rub the chicken inside and out with the spice mixture. Let the chicken sit at room temperature for 30 to 45 minutes.

Preheat the oven to 375°F.

Place the chicken in a Dutch oven just large enough to hold it without crowding and pour the milk into the bottom of the pot. Add the garlic head, bay leaf, and lemon zest to the pot. Place the pot over medium-high heat and bring the milk just to a simmer.

Transfer the pot to the oven and roast the chicken until the meat is very tender and beginning to fall off the bones, about 1½ hours. The milk might curdle and separate, but that's fine. Remove the pot from the oven and transfer the chicken to a carving board. Let the chicken rest for about 10 minutes. Remove and discard the garlic and bay leaf from the sauce.

Carve the chicken and arrange the pieces on a serving platter. Reheat the sauce on the stove top and drizzle the chicken pieces with the flavorful milk sauce. Pass the lyok at the table.

Fried Chicken Livers

with Pomegranate Molasses

Смажена куряча печінка з гранатовим сиропом

SERVES 2 TO 4

2 tablespoons sunflower oil

1 large yellow onion, halved through the stem end, then cut into thin half-moons

1 pound chicken livers, rinsed, trimmed of connective tissue, and patted dry

Salt and freshly ground black pepper

½ cup all-purpose flour

2 tablespoons ghee

¼ cup Pomegranate Molasses (page 176)

¼ cup pomegranate seeds

¼ cup loosely packed fresh cilantro leaves

One of the coolest things about growing up in Ukraine is that my parents taught me from an early age to eat and appreciate dishes made with all kinds of offal. I know that for many people in the United States, chicken livers are an acquired taste. But for me, they are a real treat, especially topped with cilantro and homemade pomegranate molasses when I want to channel Georgian *supra* vibes. This dish tastes great with Hutsul polenta (page 78) and *khachapuri* (page 113) on the side. It pairs incredibly well with a great stout beer. *Budmo!*

In a medium frying pan, heat the oil over medium-high heat. Add the onion and cook, stirring occasionally, until golden brown, 15 to 20 minutes. Remove from the heat and keep warm until serving.

While the onion is cooking, lightly season the livers with salt and pepper. Put the flour into a small bowl and season it with a generous pinch of salt.

Have ready a large plate lined with paper towels. In a large frying pan, heat the ghee over medium-high heat. Working in batches to avoid crowding, dredge the chicken livers in the flour, shaking off the excess, and add to the hot ghee. Fry the livers, turning as needed, until golden brown and crispy on all sides and barely pink in the center, about 3 minutes on each side. Transfer to the prepared plate to drain. Repeat with the remaining livers.

Arrange half of the fried onion on a serving dish, top with the crispy fried livers, and drizzle with the pomegranate molasses. Top with the remaining fried onion, sprinkle with the pomegranate seeds and cilantro leaves, and serve right away.

Plov with Quail

Плов з перепілками

SERVES 8

3 cups medium-grain rice (such as Bomba or Calrose)

2 whole quail

10 ounces boneless lamb shoulder, cut into 1-inch cubes

Salt and freshly ground black pepper

½ cup sunflower oil

2 medium yellow onions, diced

2 medium carrots, peeled and cut into matchsticks ⅛ inch wide and thick

2 teaspoons ground cumin

1 teaspoon ground turmeric

1 tablespoon dried barberries (optional)

1 head garlic

2 bay leaves

6 hard-boiled quail eggs, peeled and halved lengthwise

Rumor has it that in 1945 when Roosevelt and Churchill went to the Yalta Conference to meet with Stalin to discuss the postwar reorganization of Europe, Stalin's chef served them this grand Uzbek *plov* with whole quail and quail eggs. This looks more festive than the traditional *plov*, a simple chicken and rice dish. I usually only cook this *plov* for my pop-up dinners, where I like to serve it with Mom's Famous Spicy and Sour Tomatoes (page 162) and eggplant caviar (page 57) on the side.

Put the rice into a fine-mesh sieve and rinse under cold running water until the water runs clear. Transfer the rice to a medium bowl, add water to cover, and let soak for about 2 hours.

Pat the quail and lamb dry with paper towels and season generously with salt and pepper.

In a large, round Dutch oven, heat a few tablespoons of the oil over high heat. Add the quail and fry, turning as needed, until the skin is golden brown on all sides, about 10 minutes total. Transfer the quail to a large plate.

In the same pot, heat a couple more tablespoons of the oil over high heat. Working in batches to avoid crowing, add the lamb cubes and brown, turning as needed, until deep golden on all sides, about 4 minutes total. Transfer the meat to the plate with the quail.

In the same pot, heat the remaining oil over medium heat. Add the onions and carrots and cook, stirring occasionally, until the onions are translucent, soft, and fragrant and the carrots are soft, about 12 minutes. Add the cumin, turmeric, barberries (if using), a generous pinch of salt, and a few grinds of pepper and stir to mix well. Don't be afraid to add salt. The mixture should be very salty, as it will act as the seasoning for the rice.

Return the lamb to the pot and mix it well with the vegetables. Place the quail on top of the lamb and put the garlic head and bay leaves in the center. Drain the rice and evenly spread it on top of the lamb and quail. Do not mix at any point.

Carefully pour water over the rice, using enough to cover the rice by about 1 inch. Bring everything to a simmer over medium-high heat and then cover the pot with a tight-fitting lid and turn down the heat to low. Cook until the water has completely evaporated and the rice is tender, 60 to 70 minutes. Then remove the pot from the heat and let it sit, covered, for about 10 minutes.

When ready to serve, remove the quail from the pot and carve each into four serving pieces. Evenly spread the rice on a large serving platter and top it with the quail, lamb, and vegetables, whole garlic head, and the quail eggs for a festive look.

Grandma's Roasted Duck

Бабусина запечена качка

SERVES 4 TO 6

1 whole Muscovy duck, 5 to 6 pounds

2 tablespoons kosher salt

1 tablespoon mixed whole peppercorns

1 large orange, zest grated and then fruit cut into 6 wedges

1 small bunch fresh sage

2 large Granny Smith or other green apples, halved, cored, and cut lengthwise into ½-inch-thick slices

2 large garlic cloves, smashed

If you ask me to name one family celebration that happened without my grandma's roasted duck, I wouldn't be able to recall it. This golden brown bird with crispy skin and meat so tender and delicate it barely needs a knife is a true staple in our family. Whether it's Christmas Eve, Easter Sunday, or someone's birthday, Granny's duck with apples is always on the table. She cooks it in the oven in a massive, oval cast-iron pot with a heavy lid to ensure the juices and flavors circulate inside and penetrate the meat all the way through. To update this dish a bit, I added fresh sage and grated orange zest to bring a touch of aromatic complexity to the equation. Everything else is exactly as she does it.

Remove the neck and giblets from the duck cavity and save for another use. Trim any excess fat from the cavity and tail area. Prick the duck skin all over with the tip of a sharp paring knife, being careful not to penetrate the meat. Pat the duck dry with paper towels.

In a heavy mortar, pound together the salt, peppercorns, orange zest, and sage until reduced to a paste.

Rub the duck inside and out with the sage mixture, then stuff the orange wedges into the cavity. Refrigerate the duck uncovered for at least 4 hours or preferably overnight. This will make the meat incredibly flavorful and the skin crisp. When ready to cook, remove the duck from the refrigerator and bring it to room temperature.

Preheat the oven to 350°F. Cover the bottom of a Dutch oven just large enough to hold the bird with the apple slices. Place the duck, breast side up, on the bed of apples and cover the pot.

Roast the duck until the meat is tender when pierced with a knife, 1 hour and 40 minutes to 2 hours. Then uncover the pot, raise the oven temperature to 400°F, and continue to roast until the skin is golden brown and the meat is fall-off-the-bone tender, 30 to 35 minutes longer.

Transfer the duck to a carving board and rub the skin with the garlic. Tent the duck with aluminum foil and let rest for 10 to 15 minutes.

To serve, transfer the apples to a large platter. Carve the bird, arrange the pieces on top of the apples, and serve immediately.

Easter Roasted Pork Tenderloin

Пасхальна буженина

SERVES 4

1 pork tenderloin, about 1¾ pounds

3 garlic cloves, halved lengthwise

1 tablespoon Dijon mustard, plus more for serving

1 tablespoon sunflower oil

1 teaspoon sweet paprika

1 teaspoon salt

½ teaspoon sugar

½ teaspoon cayenne pepper

½ teaspoon freshly ground black pepper

Beet and Horseradish Hot Sauce (page 167), for serving

Dijon mustard, for serving

This roasted pork tenderloin (*bujenina*) is one of the most famous Slavic cold cuts. My mom usually makes *bujenina* for big religious holidays like Easter. She serves it thinly sliced with some mustard and Beet and Horseradish Hot Sauce on the side. In an inspired fusion of Slavic and Vietnamese cuisines, I started using *bujenina* in my *báhn mì*–style sandwiches, and they became an instant hit with my family.

Preheat the oven to 350°F. With a small knife, make six cuts each ½ inch deep and ½ inch long in the pork tenderloin, spacing them evenly. Stuff a garlic clove half into each cut.

In a small bowl, combine the mustard, oil, paprika, salt, sugar, cayenne, and black pepper and mix well with a small spoon. Rub the mustard mixture evenly over the entire tenderloin, then wrap the tenderloin in a piece of aluminum foil.

Place the wrapped meat in a shallow baking dish and roast the pork for 40 minutes. Turn off the oven and let the pork rest in the hot oven for 1 hour. Then remove the pork from the oven, unwrap it, set it on a large plate, and let it cool completely.

Cover the pork and refrigerate for at least 3 hours before serving. When ready to serve, cut it into ¼-inch-thick slices and arrange them on a serving plate. Serve with the hot sauce and mustard.

Pork Shank

Braised with Sauerkraut and Beer

Рулька з кислою капустою і пивом

SERVES 4

2 bone-in pork shanks, 1 to 1½ pounds each

Salt and freshly ground black pepper

2 tablespoons sunflower oil

1 large yellow onion, diced

2 cups drained sauerkraut, homemade (page 156) or store-bought

1½ cups light beer

1 bay leaf

Beet and Horseradish Hot Sauce (page 167), for serving

Dijon mustard, for serving

My mom always makes a variation of braised pork shank for Easter. I, on the other hand, save this dish for Oktoberfest. I just love how great it tastes with sauerkraut braised in light beer. Most of the time, I use my homemade sauerkraut, but store-bought will taste just as good. The secret to making this dish is to cook the shank until the meat is super tender and starts falling off the bone. I usually serve it with a bowl of Vegetarian Russian Potato Salad (page 51) and plenty of *Kölsch*, the famed pale brew of Cologne.

Preheat the oven to 350°F.

Season the pork shanks with a good pinch of salt and a few grinds of pepper. In a large Dutch oven, heat the oil over medium-high heat. Add the pork shanks and brown, turning as needed, until deep golden on all sides, about 8 minutes. Transfer the shanks to a large plate.

Lower the heat to medium, add the onion to the pot, and cook, stirring occasionally, until translucent and soft, about 10 minutes. Add the sauerkraut, beer, and bay leaf, season with a pinch each of salt and pepper, and mix well with a wooden spoon.

Return the pork shanks to the pot, placing them on top of the sauerkraut, then cover the pot and transfer it into the oven. Braise the pork shanks until the meat is so tender it almost falls off the bone, 2 to 2½ hours.

This dish calls for a grand presentation. To serve, arrange the braised sauerkraut on a large serving plate and place the whole pork shanks on top, then carve the meat at the table. Serve with the hot sauce and mustard.

Potatoes Fried with Pork Belly

Смажена картопля

SERVES 4

2 tablespoons sunflower oil

8 ounces pork belly, cut into pieces 1 inch long and ½ inch thick

2 pounds medium Yukon Gold potatoes, peeled and cut into slices 2½ inches long and ¼ inch thick

Salt and freshly ground black pepper

1 large yellow onion, diced

I request this dish every time I visit my mom, and I literally can't get enough of it. Her secret is a perfectly seasoned cast-iron pan with a tight-fitting lid. The potato slices end up incredibly tender on the inside and with a lovely golden crust on the outside. I always eat this dish with Mom's Famous Spicy and Sour Tomatoes (page 162) and Fermented "Sour" Eggplant (page 164).

In a large, nonstick frying pan, heat the oil over medium-high heat. Add the pork belly and fry, stirring occasionally, until lightly golden, about 5 minutes. Add the potatoes, season with a good pinch each of salt and pepper, and mix well with a wooden spatula. Cover the pan, lower the heat to medium, and cook, stirring occasionally, until the potatoes are tender, about 15 minutes. Add the onion, mix well, re-cover, and continue to cook, gently tossing the potatoes with the spatula from time to time, until the potatoes and onion are very soft, about 15 minutes.

When the potatoes are ready, remove from the heat and serve immediately.

Bell Peppers

Stuffed with Meat and Rice

Фаршировані перці

SERVES 6

¾ cup medium-grain white rice
(such as Bomba or Calrose)

Salt and freshly ground
black pepper

6 medium-large red or orange
bell peppers

2 tablespoons sunflower oil

1 medium yellow onion, finely diced

1 large carrot, peeled and
coarsely grated

1 tablespoon tomato paste

2 cups canned diced tomatoes

2 cups vegetable broth or water

1 tablespoon heavy cream

1 pound ground pork

1 bay leaf

Sour cream, for serving

Stuffed bell peppers are one of the most popular dishes of Ukrainian home cooks. These peppers are easy to make, and they're very filling. When I was a kid, the delicious tomato sauce was my favorite part of the dish. I would ask for a huge bowl of just the sauce and eat it with a slice of fluffy white bread and a dollop of sour cream. When I got older, things changed. Now I eat the whole dish, not just the sauce, but white bread and sour cream are still a part of the feast.

In a small saucepan, combine the rice with water to cover by 2½ inches and a pinch of salt. Bring to a boil over medium high-heat and cook until the rice is translucent and half cooked, 10 to 15 minutes. Drain the rice and let it cool while you prepare the remaining ingredients.

Cut off the stem end of each bell pepper and remove the seeds.

In a large, deep frying pan, heat the oil over medium heat. Add the onion and carrot and cook, stirring occasionally, until the onion is translucent and the onion and carrot are soft, 8 to 10 minutes. Stir in the tomato paste and cook, stirring, for 1 minute. Add the canned tomatoes and broth, stir well, and raise the heat to medium-high. Bring the sauce to a simmer and stir in the cream. Season the sauce with salt and pepper and remove from the heat.

In a medium bowl, mix together the pork and parboiled rice and season with a generous pinch each of salt and pepper. To check the seasoning, make a tiny patty (1 tablespoon will be enough), fry it in a small frying pan over medium heat, and taste. Add more seasoning to the remaining mixture if needed. Tightly stuff the peppers with the filling.

Stand the stuffed pepper in a pot just large enough to hold them in a single layer without crowding and carefully pour in the sauce. Make sure the sauce completely covers the peppers. Add the bay leaf to the pot, place the pot over medium-high heat, and bring the sauce to a boil. Turn down the heat to medium-low and simmer until the peppers are soft and the meat filling is no longer pink in the center, about 40 minutes.

Transfer the peppers to individual plates and spoon the tomato sauce over the top, discarding the bay leaf. Serve with the sour cream.

Crimean Beef Stew with Chickpeas

Кримська печеня з яловичини

SERVES 6 TO 8

1 cup dried chickpeas, rinsed and picked over

5 cups water

2 pounds boneless beef chuck, cut into 1½-inch pieces

Salt and freshly ground black pepper

⅓ cup sunflower oil, or more if needed

1 large yellow onion, diced

1 (28-ounce) can diced tomatoes, with their liquid

½ cup dry white wine

1 teaspoon sugar

½ teaspoon ground coriander

½ teaspoon ground fenugreek

½ teaspoon red chile flakes

6 garlic cloves, minced

½ cup loosely packed fresh cilantro leaves, plus more for serving

Pickled Red Onion (page 160), for serving

I tried this hearty, delicious stew many years ago in a small Tatar restaurant during one of my many trips to Crimea. After Russia annexed Crimea, I never had a chance to return there and get the recipe, so I re-created the dish from my memory, and I'm very pleased with how it turned out. The aromatic spices, refreshing cilantro, and bright pickled onion all come together in a beautiful symphony, complementing the meat without overpowering it. Serve this stew with a side of buttery rice and some pickled tomatoes (page 162), and I promise you everyone will ask for seconds.

Put the chickpeas into a medium bowl, add 4 cups of the water, and leave to soak at room temperature overnight.

The next day, pat the meat dry with paper towels and season generously with salt. In a large Dutch oven, heat the oil over medium-high heat. Working in batches to avoid crowding, add the meat and brown, turning as needed, until nice and golden on all sides, about 1 minute on each side. Transfer to a large plate and repeat with the remaining meat, adding more oil if needed.

When all the meat is browned, add the onion to the pot, lower the heat to medium, and cook, stirring occasionally, until translucent and soft, about 10 minutes. Return the meat to the pot and add the tomatoes, wine, and the remaining 1 cup water. Raise the heat to medium-high, bring the stew to a boil, and then lower the heat to medium-low. Stir in the sugar, coriander, fenugreek, and chile flakes and season with salt and pepper. Cover and simmer until the meat is very tender, about 1½ hours.

Meanwhile, drain the chickpeas, transfer them to a medium saucepan, and add water to cover by about 2 inches. Bring to a boil over medium-high heat and cook until soft but not mushy, about 40 minutes. Drain and reserve.

When the meat is very tender, add the chickpeas and garlic to the pot, stir well, and simmer for 5 more minutes to merge the favors, adding more water to the pot if needed to thin to a good stew consistency. Stir in the cilantro, then taste and adjust the seasoning with salt and pepper if needed. Simmer for just 3 more minutes to blend the flavors, then remove from the heat.

Serve the stew topped with the pickled onion and cilantro.

BREADS, CREPES, AND DUMPLINGS

ХЛІБ, МЛИНЦІ, ТА ВАРЕНИКИ

EASTERN EUROPEAN, and particularly Ukrainian, cuisine is famous for its dumplings, blini, crepes, and all kinds of sweet and savory breads. These dishes have always been a part of the daily table and have also traditionally been served for large gatherings and for religious celebrations, such as Christmas and Easter.

In Slavic culture, almost every holiday has a dedicated pastry, blini, or dumpling dish. For example, in Ukraine, we usually make *pelmeni* (Russian meat dumplings) for the New Year celebration, *varenyky* for Christmas Eve, and stacks of crepes for Maslenitsa, the last week before Great Lent.

In this chapter, I have featured the most beloved and joyful dough- and batter-based dishes from all corners of Eastern Europe. Among them are *varenyky*, Ukraine's national dumplings; yeasted Russian barley blini; *chebureki*, crispy Crimean turnovers; and splendid Adjarian *khachapuri*, flatbreads oozing with cheese and butter. Some recipes, like thick and fluffy Ukrainian *oladky* (pancakes) and airy Hungarian *lángos* (fried bread) are quick and easy to make. Others, like rye *pelmeni* and *khachapuri*, require more time and patience. But don't be so intimidated that you fail to try something that is time-consuming, because at the end, you'll be rewarded with an incredible result.

Adjarian Khachapuri

Хачапурі по-аджарські

MAKES 2 FLATBREADS
SERVES 2 TO 4

1¼ cups whole milk, heated to lukewarm (110° to 115°F)

1 teaspoon active dry yeast

¾ teaspoon sugar

3 cups all-purpose flour, plus more for dusting

Kosher salt

1 tablespoon sunflower oil, plus more for brushing the dough

9 ounces low-moisture mozzarella cheese, shredded (about 2¼ cups)

5 ounces whole-milk ricotta cheese (½ cup)

2 egg yolks

2 tablespoons unsalted butter, at room temperature

This book would not be complete without this lavish flatbread filled with cheese, butter, and egg from the Adjara region of Georgia. It looks impressive, but it's much easier to make than you might think, and I guarantee everyone will be wowed by both its look and, most importantly, its fantastic flavor and texture. Make it for your friends and family and serve it with Rustic Vegetable Salad with Walnut Dressing (page 45), as the dressing helps to balance the richness of the bread. You could even throw a small Georgian *supra* if you can find a bottle of a Qvevri orange wine from the wine region of Kakheti. *Gaumarjos!* Also, please don't call *khachapuri* Georgian pizza.

In a large bowl, whisk together the milk, yeast, and sugar. Cover the bowl with a kitchen towel and let stand until bubbly and foamy, 5 to 10 minutes.

Sift the flour into the yeast mixture, add ¾ teaspoon salt and the oil, and, using a rubber spatula, stir until well combined and a rough dough comes together. Transfer the dough to a clean work surface and knead until the dough comes together in a ball, then continue kneading until the dough is slightly sticky and soft, about 5 minutes.

Divide the dough in half and shape each half into a ball. Lightly brush the balls with oil and then put each ball into a large ziplock plastic bag and seal closed or into a medium bowl and cover the bowls with plastic wrap. Let the dough rest in a warm place (70° to 80°F) until it doubles in size, about 1½ hours.

Line a large sheet pan with parchment paper. In a small bowl, mix together the mozzarella and ricotta. Season with a pinch of salt and stir to combine. Set aside.

When the dough balls have doubled in size, transfer them to a lightly floured work surface. Roll out each ball into an oval about 10 inches long, 7 inches wide, and ¼ inch thick. Spread about one-fourth of the cheese mixture over each oval, leaving a 1½-inch border uncovered all the way around. Working with one oval at a time, fold the two long sides in to meet in the center and pinch the edges together tightly to seal. Flip the dough over so the side with the pinched seam is now facing down. Using a small, sharp knife, make a lengthwise cut down the center of the dough, stopping within 1½ inches of each narrow end. Tucking the long sides of the shaped dough under and away from the center, roll the edges to form the shape of a boat. There will be cheese sealed inside the rolled edges. Repeat with the second dough oval. Divide the remaining cheese mixture evenly between the two "boats," placing it in the middle of each "boat" and then lightly pressing it down.

Carefully transfer the flatbreads to the prepared pan, spacing them a few inches apart, and cover with a kitchen towel. Let rest in a warm place (70° to 80°F) until slightly puffed, 15 to 30 minutes. Meanwhile, preheat the oven to 400°F.

Bake the flatbreads, rotating the sheet pan back to front halfway through baking, until the crust is golden brown, about 25 minutes. Remove from the oven. Using the back of a spoon, make a well in the center of each flatbread and drop an egg yolk into each well. Return the flatbreads to the oven and bake until the yolks are set but are still nice and liquid, 30 to 40 seconds.

Transfer the flatbreads to a serving platter, top each one with half of the butter, and serve right away.

Spread about one-fourth of the cheese mixture over each oval or rolled dough, leaving a 1½-inch border uncovered.

Fold the two long sides in to meet in the center and pinch the edges together tightly to seal.

Flip the dough over and place it seam side down.

Make a lengthwise cut down the center of the dough, stopping within 1½ inches of each narrow end.

Tuck the long sides of the dough under and away from the center, roll the edges to form the shape of a boat.

Top the dough with more of the cheese mixture.

Garlic Pampushky

Пампушки з часником

MAKES 16 ROLLS
SERVES 8

1 cup whole milk, heated to lukewarm (110° to 115°F)

2 teaspoons sugar

1½ teaspoons active dry yeast

2 eggs

5 tablespoons sunflower oil, plus more for oiling the bowl and baking dishes

3 cups all-purpose flour (see Note)

2 teaspoons salt

4 garlic cloves, minced

2 tablespoons chopped fresh dill

Flaky sea salt, for topping

note: The dough should be very soft and barely sticky. If it feels too sticky as you knead, add 1 to 2 tablespoons flour. If it seems a bit sticky when you begin forming the balls, lightly oil your hands.

I'm a big believer that garlic makes everything taste better. This bread is living proof of my theory. When served plain, which actually never happens in Ukraine, *pampushky* are just regular boring dinner rolls. But a few cloves of minced garlic mixed with oil and fresh dill transform them into a delightful Ukrainian treat called *pampushky z chasnykom*. *Pampushky* and borscht are the most classic Ukrainian food combination, dating back hundreds of years. Ukrainians even have a saying about it: If a woman cooks borscht for a man, it means she likes him. If she serves the borscht with garlic *pampushky*, she is in love. As a true son of his country, my husband refuses to eat his borscht without freshly made *pampushky* topped with lots of garlic. It might sound whimsical, but I see it as the purest form of culinary patriotism. Or maybe he just wants to make sure I still love him dearly.

In a large bowl, whisk together the milk, sugar, and yeast. Let stand until foamy and bubbly, 5 to 10 minutes.

Crack one of the eggs into the yeast mixture, then add 3 tablespoons of the oil, the flour, and the salt. Using a rubber spatula, stir until well mixed and a rough dough comes together. Using your hands, knead the dough in the bowl until soft, supple, and pliable, 1 to 2 minutes. Add a little more flour if the dough feels too sticky (see Note). Shape the dough into a ball.

Lightly oil a second large bowl and put the dough into it. Cover the bowl with plastic wrap and let the dough rise in a warm place (70° to 80°F) until doubled in size, about 1 hour.

Oil two 9-inch square baking dishes. Turn the dough out onto a clean work surface and divide it into sixteen equal portions. Form each portion into a ball. Arrange half of the balls in each prepared baking dish, spacing them ½ inch apart. Cover each dish with a kitchen towel and let the dough rise again in a warm place until doubled in size, about 30 minutes.

Preheat the oven to 350°F. In a small bowl, lightly beat the remaining egg.

Brush the top of each roll with the egg. Bake the rolls until they are a deep golden brown, 35 to 45 minutes.

While the rolls are baking, in a small bowl, mix together the remaining 2 tablespoons oil, the garlic, and the dill.

When the rolls are ready, remove from the oven and immediately brush each roll with the garlic oil and top with a tiny pinch of flaky salt. Transfer the rolls to wire racks and let cool before serving. These rolls taste best the day they are baked.

Lángos

with Salmon Roe and Sour Cream

Лангош зі сметаною та ікрою

**MAKES 4 FLATBREADS
SERVES 2**

¾ cup whole milk, heated to lukewarm (110° to 115°F)

1 teaspoon active dry yeast

1 teaspoon sugar

1½ cups all-purpose flour, plus more for dusting

½ teaspoon salt

Sunflower oil, for oiling your hands and for frying

½ cup sour cream

2 tablespoons chopped fresh dill

Salmon roe, for serving

This traditional flatbread is a favorite street food in Hungary. Vendors deep-fry the light, fluffy rounds to order and serve them piping hot simply rubbed with garlic or smothered with shredded cheese, ketchup, onion, and bacon. My version is served the Ukrainian way, topped with dill-laced sour cream and salmon roe, for a more sophisticated presentation.

In a small bowl, whisk together the milk, yeast, and sugar. Let stand until bubbly and foamy, 5 to 10 minutes.

In a medium bowl, stir together the flour and salt. Pour in the yeast mixture and mix well with a rubber spatula until a slightly sticky, soft dough forms. Lightly oil your hands and continue mixing the dough in the bowl until it is soft and smooth, about 5 minutes longer. Cover the bowl with plastic wrap and let the dough rise in a warm place (70° to 80°F) until it doubles in size, 40 to 50 minutes.

Gently punch down the dough to release the air, re-cover the bowl, and let the dough rise again until it almost doubles in size, about 30 minutes.

Transfer the dough to a generously floured work surface and lightly dust it with flour. Divide the dough into four equal portions and shape each portion into a ball. Don't knead the dough, as you want to keep it as delicate as possible. Cover the balls with a kitchen towel and let rest at room temperature for 10 minutes.

While the dough rests, in a small bowl, stir together the sour cream and dill and set aside.

Have ready a large plate lined with paper towels. Pour the oil to a depth of 1 inch into a large, deep frying pan and heat over medium-high heat to 325°F. Using your hands, gently stretch one of the dough balls into a pancake about 5 inches in diameter and ¾ inch thick. Carefully place it in the hot oil and fry, turning once, until golden brown on both sides, about 2 minutes on each side. Transfer the flatbread to the prepared plate to drain and repeat with the other dough balls.

Serve immediately topped with dollops of the dilled sour cream and salmon roe.

Crispy Potato Kremzlyky

Кремзлики

SERVES 2 TO 4

1½ pounds Yukon Gold potatoes, peeled

1 yellow onion, about 6 ounces

1 teaspoon salt

¼ teaspoon freshly ground black pepper

1 tablespoon cornstarch

Sunflower or canola oil, for frying

½ cup sour cream, for serving

1 tablespoon minced fresh chives, for serving

Kremzlyky is the Ukrainian name for Jewish latkes aka potato pancakes. It's also one of my favorite savory brunch dishes. I usually serve them with plenty of sour cream and topped with luscious salmon roe or thinly sliced Cured Salmon (page 35). Here I have finished them with just sour cream and chives. *Kremzlyky* are easy to make and require only a handful of ingredients. I grate the potatoes and onion very finely and use just a bit of cornstarch to bind the batter. I never add any flour or egg. This method makes the flavor and texture especially good. My only advice is always to use a nonstick pan!

Using the small holes on a box grater, finely grate the potatoes and onion. The consistency should be slightly coarser than a puree. Put the grated vegetables into a large fine-mesh sieve and, holding the sieve over the sink, lightly press against the vegetables with a large spoon to drain off as much moisture as possible. Transfer the vegetables to a medium bowl and stir in the salt, pepper, and cornstarch to finish the batter.

Have ready a large plate lined with paper towels. In a large, nonstick frying pan, heat ¼ cup oil over medium heat until hot and shimmering. Scoop up about 2 tablespoons of the batter with a large spoon, add it to the hot pan, and gently flatten it with the back of the spoon to form a round pancake. Repeat with additional batter, being careful not to crowd the pan. Fry the pancakes, turning once, until golden and crisp on both sides, 2 to 3 minutes on each side. Transfer them to the prepared plate and keep warm. Repeat with the remaining batter, adding more oil to the pan as needed.

Serve the pancakes hot, topped with the sour cream and chives.

Chebureki

with Ground Meat and Caraway Seeds

Чебуреки

MAKES 8 TURNOVERS
SERVES 4

FOR THE DOUGH

2 cups all-purpose flour,
plus more for dusting

1 teaspoon sugar

½ teaspoon salt

½ cup plus 1 tablespoon water

1½ tablespoons sunflower or
canola oil, plus more for the bowl

1½ tablespoons vodka

FOR THE FILLING

8 ounces ground meat (such as
pork, beef, or chicken, or equal
parts pork and beef)

1 medium yellow onion, finely grated

⅓ cup cold water

1 teaspoon salt

½ teaspoon ground caraway seeds

½ teaspoon freshly ground
black pepper

¼ teaspoon granulated garlic

Sunflower or other neutral oil with
high-smoke point, for frying

Green Raw Ajika (page 168),
for serving

Chebureki were the quintessential Soviet street food, adored by kids and adults alike. I remember buying the piping-hot turnovers wrapped in a piece of newspaper on my way home from school. I did it so often that my mom started making them because she worried that the local vendor was using questionable ingredients. She was probably right. To this day, every time she comes to visit, we get together in the kitchen and make a batch of delightfully crisp and juicy beef-and-pork *chebureki*. Our family secret is the addition of a little vodka to the dough, which makes it fry up light and bubbly.

To make the dough, in a large bowl, stir together the flour, sugar, and salt. Make a well in the center and pour the water, oil, and vodka into the well. Using a fork, gradually draw the flour mixture into the water mixture and mix until the dough comes together in a shaggy mass. Transfer the dough to a lightly floured work surface and knead until smooth and elastic, about 5 minutes. Shape the dough into a ball. Oil a medium bowl, place the dough in it, cover the bowl with plastic wrap, and let the dough rest at room temperature for 30 minutes.

Meanwhile, make the filling. In a medium bowl, combine all the ingredients and mix well. The mixture should have the consistency of thin yogurt.

Transfer the dough to a lightly floured work surface and divide the dough into eight equal portions. Working with one portion at a time and keeping the others covered, roll out the dough into a round ⅛ inch thick. Using a plate 7 to 8 inches in diameter as a template, invert it onto the dough and trace around the edge with a small knife. Lift off the plate and pull away the dough scraps. Place 2 to 3 tablespoons of the filling on half of the round, spreading it evenly and leaving a ½-inch border uncovered. Lightly brush the border with water and fold over the other half of the dough, forming a half-moon. Press the edges with a fork to seal. Repeat with the remaining dough portions and filling.

Have ready a large plate lined with paper towels. Pour the oil to a depth of 1 inch into a large, deep frying pan and heat over medium-high heat to 350°F. Add as many turnovers to the hot oil as will fit without crowding and fry, turning once, until they are a deep golden color on both sides, 3 to 4 minutes on each side. Transfer to the prepared plate. Repeat with the remaining turnovers, adding more oil to the pan as needed.

Serve the turnovers right away with the ajika.

Panfried Bilyashi

with Chicken and Green Onion

Біляші з куркою і зеленою цибулею

Pyrizhky Dough (recipe follows)

FOR THE FILLING

1 pound ground dark-meat chicken

⅔ cup finely chopped green onions, white and green parts

1½ teaspoons salt

½ teaspoon freshly ground black pepper

Sunflower oil, for frying

These turnovers are one of the many variations of Eastern European *pyrizhky*. They are stuffed with ground chicken and a lot of finely chopped green onion, a combination that works exceptionally well. My only advice is to roll the dough a little thinner than for regular *pyrizhky*. That way, you'll make sure that the filling is cooked all the way through.

Make the dough as directed and transfer it to a lightly floured work surface. Divide it into twelve equal portions and roll each portion into a ball. Cover the balls with a kitchen towel.

To make the filling, in a medium bowl, combine all the ingredients and mix well.

Clean the work surface and dust again with flour. Place a ball on the floured surface and roll it out into a round about 4½ inches in diameter and ¼ inch thick. Place 2 heaping tablespoons of the filling in the center of the round. Fold the dough round in half to enclose the filling and pinch the edges together to seal. Lightly press the pastry with your palm to flatten it and give it a circular shape. It should be about ½ inch thick. Repeat with the remaining dough balls and filling.

Have ready a large plate lined with paper towels. Pour the oil to a depth of 1 inch into a large, deep frying pan and heat over medium-high heat to 325°F. Carefully place one or two pastries in the hot oil, being careful not to crowd the pan, and fry, turning once, until golden brown on both sides, 2 to 3 minutes on each side. Lower the heat to medium-low if you feel the pastry is cooking too fast. You need to make sure the meat filling is fully cooked. Transfer the pastry to the prepared plate and repeat with the remaining pastries.

Serve the pyrizhky hot or at room temperature.

Pyrizhky Dough

ENOUGH FOR 12 TO 14 SMALL PASTRIES OR 4 TO 6 LARGER PASTRIES

2 cups whole milk, heated to lukewarm (110° to 115°F)

2 tablespoons sugar

1½ teaspoons active dry yeast or instant yeast

3¼ cups all-purpose flour, plus more for dusting

1 teaspoon salt

Sunflower oil, for oiling your hands and the bowl

In a small bowl, whisk together the milk, sugar, and yeast. Let stand until foamy and bubbly, 5 to 10 minutes.

In a large bowl, stir together the flour and salt. Pour in the yeast mixture and mix well with a rubber spatula until a slightly sticky, soft dough comes together. Lightly oil your hands and knead the dough in the bowl until it is smooth, soft, and not too sticky, about 4 minutes. Shape the dough into a ball.

Lightly oil a second large bowl and put the dough into it. Cover the bowl with plastic wrap and let the dough rise in a warm place (70° to 80°F) until doubled in size, 50 to 60 minutes. Use as directed in individual recipes.

Fried Flatbread

with Eggs and Herbs

Пироги з яйцем і зеленню

SERVES 4 TO 6

Pyrizhky Dough (page 125)

FOR THE FILLING

8 hard-boiled eggs, peeled and cut into ¼-inch cubes

1½ cups tightly packed chopped fresh dill, flat-leaf parsley, and green onions (white and green parts), in roughly equal parts

Salt and freshly ground black pepper

About 6 tablespoons sunflower oil, for frying

½ cup sour cream, for serving

This is my take on traditional Ukrainian savory *pyrizhky*. Instead of making a dozen or so small pastries, I decided to make a few large flatbreads and stuff them generously with herbs and chopped eggs. They make a wholesome meal served with Golden Beet Vinegret Salad (page 48) or beet *pkhali* (page 52).

Make the dough as directed and transfer it to a lightly floured work surface. Divide it into four to six equal portions, depending on the number of servings or size desired. Cover the balls with a kitchen towel and let rest for 10 minutes.

Meanwhile, make the filling. In a medium bowl, combine the eggs and herbs, season with a generous pinch each of salt and pepper, and mix well.

On a lightly floured work surface, roll out a dough ball into a round 7 to 8 inches in diameter and ¼ inch thick. Place a generous amount of filling in the center of the round (the amount will depend on the number of flatbreads you are making). Fold the edges of the round toward the center to cover the filling and press the edges together to seal. No filling should be visible. Lightly press on the pastry with your palm to make it flat and round again. It should be about ¾ inch thick. Repeat with the remaining dough balls and filling.

Have ready a large plate lined with paper towels. In a large frying pan, heat 2 tablespoons of the oil over medium heat. When the oil is hot, place a flatbread in the pan and lower the heat to medium-low. Fry the flatbread, turning once, until golden brown on both sides, about 4 minutes on each side. Transfer the flatbread to the prepared plate. Repeat with the remaining flatbreads, adding more oil to the pan as needed.

Serve the flatbreads warm or at room temperature.

Chicken and Mushroom Crepes

Млинці з куркою та грибами

Crepes (recipe follows; see note)

FOR THE FILLING

2 tablespoons sunflower oil

1 medium yellow onion, chopped

8 ounces mushrooms (such as white, button, cremini, or portobello), thinly sliced

1 pound ground dark-meat chicken

¼ cup sour cream

3 tablespoons chopped green onion, green part only

2 tablespoons sunflower oil

Salt and freshly ground black pepper

16 long green onion leaves, for serving

Sour cream, for serving

Here, my mom's legendary thin, buttery crepes enclose a savory filling. She usually makes this version for family gatherings and special occasions; the bundles are tied at the top with a length of green onion, which makes them look especially festive and cute on the table.

Make the crepe batter as directed.

While the batter is resting, make the filling. In a large sauté pan, heat the oil over medium-high heat. Add the yellow onion and cook, stirring occasionally, until the onion is translucent and soft, about 7 minutes. Add the mushrooms and cook, stirring occasionally, until the mushrooms are soft, about 7 minutes. Add the chicken and cook, breaking up any large chunks with a wooden spatula, until the meat is cooked through and no longer pink, 3 to 5 minutes. Stir in the sour cream and green onion and season to taste with salt and pepper. Transfer the filling to a medium bowl and set aside to cool.

While the filling cools, cook the crepes as directed.

To assemble each crepe, place 2 to 3 tablespoons of the filling on the center of the crepe. Gather the edges of the crepe up and around the filling, creating a "beggar's purse." Wrap a long green onion leaf around the top and tie in a loose knot to secure closed. Arrange the bundles on a platter and serve right away.

Crepes

MAKES FOURTEEN TO SIXTEEN 10-INCH CREPES

2 cups all-purpose flour

3 tablespoons sugar

¾ teaspoon salt

1½ cups whole milk, at room temperature

1½ cups water, at room temperature

4 eggs

4 tablespoons unsalted butter, melted and cooled

1 teaspoon sunflower or canola oil, or more if needed, for cooking

In a medium bowl, stir together the flour, sugar, and salt. In a large bowl, whisk together the milk, water, and eggs. While continuing to whisk constantly, gradually add the flour mixture to the milk mixture. When all of the flour mixture is incorporated, continue to whisk until you have a smooth batter with a consistency slightly thicker than that of heavy cream. Pour in the butter and give the batter a good stir. Cover the bowl with plastic wrap and let the batter rest at room temperature for at least 30 minutes or up to 2 hours before cooking the crepes.

Preheat a 10-inch nonstick frying pan over medium heat. Before frying the first crepe, lightly brush the hot pan with the oil to make sure the crepe doesn't stick. Give the batter a good stir with a whisk right before you begin cooking. Using a ladle, pour a small amount of the batter (about ½ cup) into the hot pan and immediately rotate the pan to spread the batter as thinly as possible. Cook the crepe over medium heat until lightly browned on the edges, about 1 minute. Loosen the edges of the crepe with a spatula, flip the crepe over, and cook on the second side until lightly golden, 20 to 30 seconds. Transfer the crepe to a warmed platter and repeat the same steps with the remaining batter, stacking the crepes as they emerge from the pan and covering them with a kitchen towel to keep them warm. If your crepes begin to stick to the pan, brush the pan with a little more oil.

note: The batter can be made up to a day in advance and refrigerated. Bring it to room temperature before cooking the crepes.

Sauerkraut and Potato Varenyky

Вареники з картоплею та квашеною капустою

SERVES 4

FOR THE FILLING

3 medium Yukon Gold potatoes, about 12 ounces total weight, peeled and cut into 1-inch cubes

Salt and freshly ground black pepper

2 tablespoons sunflower oil

1 small yellow onion, finely chopped

1 cup sauerkraut, homemade (page 156) or store-bought

2 tablespoons sour cream

Varenyk Dough (recipe follows)

FOR THE TOPPING

1 tablespoon sunflower oil

6 ounces skinless pork belly, cut into 1-inch pieces

Sour cream, for serving

As you learned early in this book (see page 23), Ukrainian dumplings, or *varenyky*, are in the shadow of the much better know Polish pierogi. We cook *varenyky* in salted boiling water (the name comes from the word *varyty*, "to boil") and then usually toss them with onions fried in some kind of fat, such as oil, butter, or pork fat. But my favorite way to serve them is with *shkvarky*, small pieces of pork belly fried to crackly perfection. Dumplings and crispy pork belly are pure comfort food to me. Also, whenever I have leftover *varenyky*, I always fry them the next day in some pork fat until they develop a delicious golden brown skin, and then I eat them with a glass of tangy kefir to balance the richness.

To make the filling, in a medium saucepan, combine the potatoes with water to cover by 2 inches and a good pinch of salt and bring to a boil over high heat. Lower the heat to medium and cook until the potatoes are easily pierced with a knife, 15 to 20 minutes. Drain the potatoes and pass them through a potato ricer into a medium bowl. Or transfer them to a medium bowl and mash with a masher until smooth. Set aside.

In a medium frying pan, heat the oil over medium-high heat. Add the onion and cook, stirring occasionally, until soft and lightly golden, about 10 minutes. Add the sauerkraut and cook, stirring, until the sauerkraut is soft, about 15 minutes.

Remove from the heat and transfer to the bowl with the potatoes. Add the sour cream and, using a rubber spatula, mix everything together well. Season to taste with salt and pepper, then let the filling cool to room temperature.

While the filling cools, make the dough as directed and let rest for 30 minutes.

While the dough rests, make the topping. In a large frying pan, heat the oil over medium-high heat. Add the pork belly and fry, stirring occasionally, until deeply golden and crispy on the outside, about 15 minutes. Transfer the pork belly and the melted fat to a small heatproof bowl and set aside until needed.

Unwrap the dough and place it on a lightly floured work surface. Divide the dough in half. Roll out the other dough half into a large round ⅛ inch thick. Using a 3-inch round cookie cutter or overturned glass, cut out as many dough rounds as possible. Lift away any dough scraps and set aside. Cover the dough rounds with a kitchen towel to prevent them from drying out. Roll out the remaining dough half and cut out more rounds the same way. Press together all the dough scraps, roll out, and cut out more rounds.

Lightly dust a large sheet pan or cutting board with flour. To shape each dumpling, place a heaping tablespoon of the filling in the center of a dough round and fold the round in half to create a half-moon, being careful to press out any air and to pinch the edges to seal securely. Transfer the dumpling to the prepared pan. Repeat with the remaining rounds and filling.

When all the dumplings are shaped, bring a large pot of salted water to a boil. Drop the dumplings into the boiling water, stir them gently with a spoon to prevent them from sticking together, and cook for 5 to 7 minutes. When they are plump and floating on top, they're done. Using a wire skimmer or other broad slotted utensil, fish the dumplings out of the water and drop them into a large bowl.

Top the dumplings with the fried pork belly and drizzle with a couple of tablespoons of the fat. Serve right away with sour cream on the side.

Varenyk Dough

ENOUGH FOR 36 TO 42 DUMPLINGS

3 cups all-purpose flour, plus more for dusting

1 teaspoon salt

1 whole egg

1 egg yolk

¾ cup water

1 tablespoon sunflower oil

In a large bowl, stir together the flour and salt. Make a well in the center of the flour and add the whole egg, egg yolk, water, and oil to the well. Carefully whisk the egg mixture with a fork until combined. Then, using the fork, gradually draw the flour into the egg mixture and mix until the dough comes together in a shaggy mass.

Transfer the dough to a lightly floured work surface and knead until smooth, about 5 minutes. Shape the dough into a ball, wrap it in plastic wrap, and let rest at room temperature for about 30 minutes. The dough can also be refrigerated for up to 6 hours and then brought to room temperature before rolling it out. Use as directed in individual recipes.

Rye Pelmeni

with Brown Butter and Spicy Herb Sauce

Ржані пельмені

SERVES 4

FOR THE BROWN BUTTER

½ cup unsalted butter, cubed
(see Note)

FOR THE DOUGH

2 cups all-purpose flour, plus
more for dusting

¼ cup dark rye flour

1 teaspoon salt

2 eggs

2 tablespoons sour cream

⅓ cup water

FOR THE SAUCE

1 small shallot, finely chopped

3 tablespoons champagne vinegar

1 small Fresno chile, finely chopped

½ cup minced fresh cilantro

¼ cup minced fresh dill

⅓ cup sunflower oil

Salt

FOR THE FILLING

6 ounces ground beef

6 ounces ground pork

1 large yellow onion, finely grated
or pureed in a food processor

1 teaspoon salt

1 teaspoon freshly ground
black pepper

Sour cream, for serving

Celery salt, for serving (optional)

Pelmeni are Russian dumplings filled with ground pork or beef mixed with onion and seasoned usually with only salt and pepper. These dumplings came to Russia from Asian nomadic tribes and are considered a close relative of Chinese *jiaozi*. *Pelmeni* are traditionally drizzled with melted butter right after boiling and are served with white vinegar on the side to cut the richness of the fatty meat filling. In my version of *pelmeni*, I have strived to find the perfect balance of rich, spicy, and acidic elements to pay homage to the original recipe while elevating the flavor and the visual appearance. I use dark rye flour to make the texture of the dough slightly more chewy, brown butter to add complex richness, and a spicy herb sauce made with champagne vinegar for the desired acidity and vibrancy. All these changes have created a particularly harmonious flavor that has made this dish a favorite in our house. To elevate the dish even further, I recommend serving the *pelmeni* with full-fat sour cream lightly dusted with celery salt for extra oomph.

To make the brown butter, place a small, heavy saucepan over medium heat. Add the butter and allow it to melt, stirring it constantly to keep it moving. Once it has melted, the butter will begin to foam and sizzle around the edges. Keep stirring. In roughly 6 to 8 minutes, the butter will turn a deep amber, with brown specs of the milk solids at the bottom of the pan, and will smell nutty and caramel-like. Remove the pan from the heat and pour the butter into a small, heatproof glass or metal bowl. Set aside until needed, or let the butter cool and solidify, then refrigerate for later use. Warm until melted before using.

To make the dough, in a large bowl, stir together both flours and the salt. Make a well in the center of the flour mixture and add the eggs, sour cream, and water to the well. Carefully whisk the egg mixture with a fork until combined. Then, using the fork, gradually draw the flour mixture into the egg mixture and mix until the dough comes together in a shaggy mass. Transfer the dough to a lightly floured work surface and knead for a few minutes until smooth. Shape the dough into a ball, wrap it in plastic wrap, and let rest at room temperature for 30 minutes. The dough can also be refrigerated for up to 6 hours and then brought to room temperature before rolling it out.

While the dough rests, make the sauce. In a small bowl, combine the shallot and vinegar and let stand for 20 to 30 minutes. Drain the shallot into a fine-mesh sieve placed over a small bowl. In a food processor, combine the shallot, chile, cilantro, dill, oil, and 2 tablespoons of the reserved vinegar and pulse just until a chunky mixture forms. Transfer the sauce to a bowl and season to taste with salt and the remaining vinegar if needed. The sauce should be used within 2 hours.

Unwrap the dough and place it on a lightly floured work surface. Divide the dough in half. Set half aside and cover with a kitchen towel. Roll out the other dough half into a large round ⅛ inch thick. Using a 2¼-inch round cookie cutter or overturned glass, cut out as many dough rounds as possible. Lift away any dough scraps and set aside. Cover the dough rounds with a kitchen towel to prevent them from drying out. Roll out the remaining dough half and cut out more rounds the same way. Press together all the dough scraps, roll out, and cut out more rounds. Cover all the dough rounds with a kitchen towel.

To make the filling, in a medium bowl, combine all the ingredients and mix well with a spoon.

Lightly dust a large sheet pan or cutting board with flour. To shape each dumpling, place 1 to 2 teaspoons of the filling in the center of a dough round and fold the round in half to create a half-moon, being careful to press out any air and to press the edges to seal securely. Bring together two corners and pinch them together with your fingers to seal. Transfer the dumpling to the prepared pan. Repeat with the remaining dough rounds and filling. As you work, keep the shaped dumplings covered with a kitchen towel.

When all the dumplings are shaped, bring a large pot of salted water to a boil. Drop the dumplings into the boiling water, stir them gently with a spoon to prevent them from sticking together, and cook for 5 to 6 minutes. When they are plump and floating on top, they're done. Using a wire skimmer or other broad slotted utensil, fish the dumplings out of the water and drop them into a large bowl. Drizzle them with a few tablespoons of the melted brown butter and gently toss to coat evenly.

Transfer the dumplings to individual plates. Top with the sauce, a dollop of sour cream, a dusting of celery salt (if using), and with more brown butter if desired. Serve right away.

Savory Tvorog Lazy Dumplings

Солоні ліниві вареники

SERVES 2

1 pound tvorog cheese, homemade (page 174) or store-bought

½ cup stinging nettle puree (see Note)

1 whole egg

1 egg yolk

½ cup grated Parmigiano-Reggiano cheese, plus more for serving

Salt and freshly ground black pepper

1 cup all-purpose flour

⅓ cup plus 2 tablespoons semolina

6 tablespoons unsalted butter, cubed

note: Young, tender nettles are sold at some farmers' markets and specialty produce stores or can be gathered in the wild. The small "spines" on the underside of the leaves and on the stems of the plants irritate the skin, so don gloves when you are working with raw nettles. Once they are cooked, the "sting" disappears. To make the nettle puree, bring a large pot of water to a rolling boil. Drop the nettles into the boiling water and blanch until the leaves are soft and bright green, about 2 minutes. Drain and immediately immerse in a large bowl of ice-cold water. Drain again and remove and discard the stems. Transfer the leaves to a blender, add a little water, and blend until a smooth puree forms. If you cannot find nettles, you can substitute spinach puree for the nettle puree.

This recipe has Italian vibes. I was so inspired by Italian light and airy ricotta dumplings that I decided to make something similar with traditional Ukrainian ingredients. We have a long history of cooking with stinging nettles in all parts of Ukraine, and I wanted to pay homage to my roots, so I have flavored the dough with a nettle puree. The puree is also a great addition to any pasta dough or cream soup.

Bring a large pot of salted water to a boil over high heat.

In a medium bowl, combine the tvorog cheese, nettle puree, whole egg, egg yolk, and Parmigiano-Reggiano cheese. Add a good pinch each of salt and pepper and mix well with a rubber spatula. Add the all-purpose flour and mix again until thoroughly incorporated. You should have soft, sticky dough.

Sprinkle a sheet pan with 2 tablespoons of the semolina. Evenly spread the remaining ⅓ cup semolina on a plate. With damp hands, scoop up a little of the dough and shape into a ball about 1¾ inches in diameter. Gently roll the ball in the semolina on the plate, coating on all sides and shaking off the excess, and then place it on the prepared pan. Repeat until all the dough is shaped.

Turn down the heat to medium-high and gently lower the dumplings into the simmering water. Cook until they float on top and are firm on the outside, about 5 minutes.

While the dumplings are cooking, transfer a couple of ladles (about 1 cup total) of the dumpling cooking water to a large frying pan and bring to a simmer over medium-high heat. Add the butter and whisk vigorously until the butter and water merge into a creamy sauce.

When the dumplings are ready, using a wire skimmer or other broad slotted utensil, fish the dumplings out of the water and place them in the creamy sauce. Simmer the dumplings in the sauce, gently tossing them with a spoon to coat them evenly in the sauce, for a few minutes.

Transfer the dumplings to a serving dish and pour the sauce remaining in the pan over the dumplings. Top with some Parmigiano-Reggiano and a few grinds of pepper. Serve immediately.

Sweet Dark Cherry Varenyky

Вареники з черешнею

SERVES 4

Varenyk Dough (page 134)

FOR THE FILLING

1½ pounds pitted fresh or thawed frozen dark cherries (from about 1¾ pounds unpitted cherries)

¼ cup granulated sugar

1 tablespoon cornstarch

1 tablespoon granulated sugar, for cooking

2 tablespoons unsalted butter, melted, for serving

2 tablespoons superfine sugar, for serving (optional)

When I was growing up in southern Ukraine, there were sour cherry trees in nearly every backyard. It broke my heart when I came to the United States and couldn't find my beloved sour cherries at any of the local farmers' markets. I still can't figure out why more people don't grow this marvelous stone fruit. Fortunately, these dumplings are amazing made with sweet dark cherries. Choose ripe medium-size fruits so you can stuff a couple of them inside each dough round and enjoy a perfect two-bite dumpling. In our family, we usually eat these sweet dumplings for lunch.

Make the dough as directed and let rest for 30 minutes.

While the dough rests, make the filling. In a medium bowl, combine all the ingredients and stir gently to mix well. Set aside.

Unwrap the dough and place it on a lightly floured work surface. Divide the dough in half. Set half aside and cover with a kitchen towel. Roll out the other dough half into a large round ⅛ inch thick. Using a 3-inch round cookie cutter or overturned glass, cut out as many dough rounds as possible. Lift away any dough scraps and set aside. Roll out the remaining dough half and cut out more rounds the same way. Press together all the dough scraps, roll out, and cut out more rounds.

Dust a large sheet pan or cutting board with flour. To shape each dumpling, place 2 cherries in the center of a dough round and fold the round in half to create a half-moon, being careful to press out any air and to pinch the edges to seal securely. Transfer the dumpling to the prepared pan. Repeat with the remaining rounds and filling.

When all the dumplings are shaped, bring a large pot of water to a rolling boil and add the granulated sugar. Drop the dumplings into the boiling water, stir them gently with a spoon to prevent them from sticking together, and cook for 5 to 7 minutes. When they are plump and floating on top, they're done. Using a wire skimmer or other broad slotted utensil, fish the dumplings out of the water and drop them into a large bowl.

Drizzle the dumplings with the butter and gently toss to coat evenly. If you want additional sweetness, sprinkle the dumplings with the superfine sugar. Serve right away.

Yeasted Barley Blini

with Creamed Honey

Пухкі млинці зі збитим медом

SERVES 4 TO 6

FOR THE BLINI

3 eggs

¼ cup sugar

½ teaspoon salt

1¼ cups whole milk, heated to lukewarm (110° to 115°F)

¾ cup lukewarm water (110° to 115°F)

1 teaspoon active dry yeast

1⅓ cups all-purpose flour

1 cup barley flour

2 tablespoons sunflower oil, plus more for frying

⅓ cup unsalted butter, melted

FOR THE CREAMED HONEY

½ cup crystallized honey

½ cup liquid honey

Blini and honey have always been a favorite duo of mine. But these fluffy barley blini with thick creamed honey took that to a whole new level of appreciation. To make creamed honey, I usually use a light and floral local California honey, such as orange blossom or clover. These blini are incredibly delicious straight from the pan, especially if brushed with melted butter. If you want to serve them with something savory, like salmon roe or cured fish, just cut the amount of sugar in the batter in half.

To make the blini batter, in a large bowl, whisk together the eggs, sugar, and salt until frothy. Pour in the milk and water and whisk until well mixed. Add the yeast and both flours and whisk everything together until no lumps remain. The batter should be the consistency of thin yogurt.

Cover the bowl with a kitchen towel and let rest for 40 minutes to activate the yeast. Then add the oil, give the batter a good stir with the whisk, re-cover, and let rest for another 10 to 15 minutes.

While the batter rests, make the creamed honey. In a stand mixer fitted with the whisk attachment, combine both honeys and beat on medium-high speed until the mixture is pale yellow and thick, about 25 minutes. Use right away, or transfer to an airtight container and store at room temperature for up to 1 month.

To cook the blini, preheat an 8-inch nonstick frying pan or crepe pan over medium-high heat until very hot. Lightly brush the bottom of the pan with oil. Pour a full ladle of the batter (about ¾ cup) into the hot pan and immediately rotate the pan to distribute the batter evenly. Cook the blini until the top is bubbly and no longer liquid and the underside is golden, about 2 minutes. Using a large spatula, flip the blini over and cook on the second side until golden, 1 to 2 minutes. Transfer the blini to a large warmed platter and brush lightly with the butter. Repeat with the remaining batter, brushing each blini with butter as it is removed from the pan and brushing the pan with more oil as needed to prevent sticking.

Serve the blini warm with the creamed honey.

Thick Kefir Oladky

Оладки

SERVES 2

1¼ cups plain kefir or buttermilk

1 egg

¼ teaspoon kosher salt

2 tablespoons sugar

½ teaspoon baking soda

1 cup all-purpose flour

Sunflower or canola oil, for frying

Honey, sour cream, and/or jam, for serving

These thick and fluffy pancakes are probably the recipe I cook the most in my kitchen. Every time I ask my husband what to make for breakfast, the answer is the same: *oladky*. I don't mind at all, as this recipe is easy to make, requires very few ingredients, and always delivers the most amazing results. Plus, there are plenty of toppings to serve with *oladky*. I love eating them with honey, my mom prefers sour cream, and my husband always asks for homemade jam. No matter what you choose, these pancakes will taste wonderful.

In a medium bowl, combine the kefir, egg, salt, sugar, and baking soda, and beat gently with a whisk. While continuing to whisk constantly, gradually add the flour. When all the flour has been added, continue to mix until the batter is smooth and thick. Let the batter rest for 15 minutes.

Have ready a large plate lined with paper towels. Pour the oil to a depth of ¼ inch into a large frying pan and heat over medium-high heat until the oil is hot and shimmering. Turn down the heat to medium-low and drop a small scoop (2 to 3 tablespoons) of the batter into the hot oil for each pancake, being careful not to crowd the pan. Cook until crisp and golden brown on the bottom and the top has set, 2 to 3 minutes. Using a spatula, flip the pancakes over and fry until crisp and golden brown on the second side, 2 to 3 minutes longer. Transfer to the prepared plate and keep warm. Repeat with the remaining batter, adding more oil to the pan as needed.

Serve the pancakes warm with your topping of choice.

Fried Apple Pyrizhky

Пиріжки з яблуками

SERVES 6 TO 8

Pyrizhky Dough (page 125)

FOR THE FILLING

1½ pounds Granny Smith apples, peeled, cored, and grated

2 tablespoons sugar, or to taste

Sunflower or canola oil, for frying

Pyrizhky (also known as *pirozhki*) are wonderful Slavic fried pastries that can be stuffed with almost any filling, both sweet and savory. My husband likes them filled with grated apples and can eat half a dozen in one sitting. I can't blame him. Once you taste these *pyrizhky*, it's incredibly hard to stop stuffing them into your mouth.

Make the dough as directed and transfer it to a lightly floured work surface.

To make the filling, in a medium bowl, combine the apples and sugar and mix well.

Roll out the dough into a large round ¼ inch thick. Using a 3½-inch round cookie cutter or overturned glass, cut out 10 to 12 dough rounds. Lift away any dough scraps and set aside. Cover the dough rounds with a kitchen towel to prevent them from drying out. Place about 2 tablespoons of the filling in the center of the round. Fold the dough round in half to enclose the filling and pinch the edges together to seal. Lightly press the pastry with your palm to flatten it and give it an oval shape. It should be about ½ inch thick. Repeat with the remaining dough balls and filling.

Have ready a large plate lined with paper towels. Pour the oil to a depth of ¼ inch into a large frying pan and heat over medium-high heat to 325°F. Carefully place a few pastries in the hot oil, being careful not to crowd the pan. Fry, turning once, until golden brown on both sides, 2 to 3 minutes on each side. Transfer the pastries to the prepared plate and repeat with the remaining pastries. Serve hot or at room temperature.

Transfer the dough to a lightly floured work surface.

Roll out the dough into a large round ¼ inch thick.

Using a 3½-inch round cookie cutter or overturned glass, cut out 10 to 12 dough rounds.

Place about 2 tablespoons of the filling in the center of the round.

Fold the dough round in half to enclose the filling and pinch the edges together to seal.

Repeat with the remaining dough balls and filling.

Sweet Cheese Fritters

Сирники

SERVES 4 TO 6

1½ pounds tvorog cheese, homemade (page 174) or store-bought

1 egg

½ cup sugar

½ teaspoon salt

1 tablespoon pure vanilla extract

¼ cup dried cherries

⅔ cup all-purpose flour, plus more for coating

Sunflower oil, for frying

Sour cream and jam, for serving

Syrnyky are the Slavic version of breakfast cheese fritters. They got their name from *syr*, the popular Ukrainian farmer's cheese. I usually make them on weekends for my husband and serve them piping hot with some homemade jam and sour cream. They make a very filling and delicious breakfast.

In a food processor, combine the cheese, egg, sugar, salt, and vanilla and process until smooth, about 1 minute.

Transfer the mixture to a medium bowl, add the cherries, and mix well. Sift the flour directly into the bowl and then mix everything together well with a rubber spatula. The mixture will come together easily but will be very soft and sticky.

Preheat the oven to 350°F. Line a sheet pan with parchment paper.

Pour the oil to a depth of ¼ inch into a large, deep frying pan and heat over medium heat. Spread a thick layer of flour on a large plate. With slightly dampened hands, shape the cheese mixture into twelve uniform balls, setting them on the floured plate as they are ready. Once all the balls are formed, dust them with more flour and then flatten each ball into a patty about 1½ inches thick and dust it generously with more flour.

Working in batches to avoid crowding, carefully place the patties in the hot oil and fry, turning once, until golden brown on both sides, 2 to 3 minutes on each side. Transfer to the prepared sheet pan. When all the fritters are fried, place the sheet pan in the oven for 5 minutes to make sure they are cooked through.

Serve the fritters immediately with sour cream and jam.

Buttery Nalysnyky

with Sweet Syr Filling

Налисники з сиром

SERVES 6 TO 8

Crepes (page 131)

FOR THE FILLING

12 ounces tvorog cheese, homemade (page 174) or store-bought

½ cup golden raisins, soaked in hot water for 30 minutes and drained

3 tablespoons sugar, or more to taste

1½ teaspoons pure vanilla extract

¼ teaspoon salt

2 tablespoons unsalted butter, melted, for brushing the crepes (optional)

This is more than a recipe. It is a family treasure. My mom is a known *nalysnyky* ninja in our family. In just a couple of hours, she can single-handedly panfry scores of paper-thin buttery crepes, spread them with filling, and roll them into perfect tubes. She makes them with dozens of different fillings, both sweet and savory. But from the time I was a small child until today, my favorite filling is creamy, tangy *tvorog* cheese with plumped raisins. I closely watched my mom's entire crepe-making process and meticulously recorded every step to create this foolproof batter recipe with just the right balance of richness and delicacy. The batter is slightly sweet, but she uses it for savory crepes as well. That's just how we roll in our family.

Make the crepe batter as directed.

While the batter is resting, make the filling. In a medium bowl, using a rubber spatula, mix together the cheese, raisins, sugar, vanilla, and salt until well blended and smooth. Set aside, or cover and refrigerate if not cooking the crepes right away.

Cook the crepes as directed.

If you crave extra richness, brush each crepe with a thin layer of melted butter while they are still warm. Then spread a thin layer of the filling on each crepe and roll it up into a tight cylinder. Serve right away. Leftover filled crepes will keep in an airtight container in the refrigerator for up to 4 days. Microwave them on high for 30 seconds to 1 minute before serving.

PICKLES, SAUCES, AND DRINKS

СОЛІННЯ, СОУСИ ТА НАПОЇ

EASTERN EUROPEAN CUISINE is shaped by seasonality, and most of the countries, including Ukraine, experience all four seasons. To survive the cold winter months, our ancestors had to preserve much of the produce gathered during the fruitful harvest season to sustain themselves through winter. And let me assure you, they mastered the craft. Slavs learned to pickle, ferment, and preserve everything that grows, and they kept those treasured jars and crocks in underground cellars, which remained cool even during the hottest days of summer.

Refrigerators arrived in Ukraine in the 1970s, and before that, many people, especially in the countryside, stored their preserves in root cellars. I still remember my grandma's cool and dark outdoor cellar—or as I called it, the dungeon—which had the steepest, tiniest steps I've ever seen in my life. I was never allowed to go there by myself, but I was always awed every time she took me with her. It looked like an underground culinary kingdom, with countless colorful jars filled with fermented tomatoes, spicy *ajika* (vegetable sauce), fizzy gherkins, fruit jams, *kompot* (fruit drink), golden mead, and more.

My grandma worked hard all summer to fill those heavily laden shelves. Every time we went there, she would let me choose a jar I wanted to open. Unlike most kids, who would have selected something sweet, I would grab a small jar of our southern-style sour eggplants to go with one of my favorite dishes, Potatoes Fried with Pork Belly (page 105). Even back then, I was a notorious pickle connoisseur.

Sauerkraut

with Caraway Seeds and Sour Cherry

Квашена капуста

1 head white cabbage, about 1½ pounds

3 tablespoons salt

1 medium carrot, peeled and shredded

1 teaspoon caraway seeds

1 tablespoon dried sour cherries

Sauerkraut is undoubtedly one of the great pillars of Eastern European cuisine. We eat it raw, braise it, boil it, and fry it. We use it to make savory pies and dumplings and add it raw into soups and stews. Because I have included a few recipes in this book that call for sauerkraut, I also decided to share my go-to homemade sauerkraut recipe. To make it extra flavorful, I always add some caraway seeds and a few dried sour cherries, but if you prefer a cleaner flavor, you can skip one or both of them.

Remove a couple of outer leaves from the cabbage. Rinse them well, pat dry with a paper towel, and set aside. Using a small, sharp knife, cut out the core from the cabbage and discard. Using a large, sharp knife, cut the cabbage in half lengthwise. Using the large knife or a mandoline, slice the cabbage halves crosswise as thinly as you can.

Put the cabbage into a large bowl and sprinkle with the salt. Using your hands, massage the cabbage until it releases plenty of water. It will take about 5 minutes. Reserve the cabbage water.

Add the carrot, caraway seeds, and cherries and mix well. Pack the cabbage mixture into a large, widemouthed glass jar and pour over all of the cabbage liquid from the bowl. Tamp down the cabbage mixture with your fist and cover the top with the reserved whole leaves. Set something heavy on top of the leaves. A quart-size plastic deli container or jar filled with salt or water works great for me. The cabbage should be fully submerged in the brine at all times.

Let the sauerkraut ferment in a cool, dark place (60° to 65°F) for about 1 week. Start tasting the cabbage on day five. When it gets to your desired flavor, remove the weight, cover the jar with a lid, and store the sauerkraut in the refrigerator for up to 6 months.

Beet Pickled Cabbage

Капуста "Пелюстка"

SERVES 6 TO 8

1 head white cabbage, about 1½ pounds

1 small red beet, about 3 ounces, peeled and cut into thin matchsticks

3 cups water

⅓ cup plus 1 tablespoon distilled white vinegar

2 bay leaves

2 garlic cloves

2 tablespoons sugar

1 tablespoon plus 1 teaspoon salt

This dish is called *pelustka,* which in Ukrainian means "petal." These beautiful cabbage pieces indeed resemble pink flower petals. Like the Beet Pickled Deviled Eggs on page 32, this is hot-pink thanks to the addition of beet. It's also super crispy, light, and vibrant. I remember going with my mom to the *bazaar* and tasting this cabbage from different vendors, picking the one that was most to my liking. Years later, I started making *pelustka* myself, but I still adjust the taste to reflect those early memories from our local Ukrainian *bazaar.*

Remove a couple of the loose outer leaf layers from the cabbage and reserve them for another use. Using a small, sharp knife, cut out the core from the cabbage and discard. Using a large, sharp knife, cut the cabbage in half lengthwise, then cut each half into roughly 2-inch square pieces. Tightly pack the chopped cabbage into a large, widemouthed heatproof glass jar with a lid.

In a small saucepan, combine the beet, water, vinegar, bay leaves, garlic, sugar, and salt and bring to a boil over medium-high heat. Adjust the heat to maintain a simmer, stirring once or twice, for 1 minute to dissolve the sugar.

Pour the hot brine over the cabbage and let cool completely. Once the mixture is at room temperature, cover the jar and refrigerate overnight. The cabbage will be ready to eat the next day. It will keep in the refrigerator for up to 1 week.

Pickled Red Onion

Маринована червона цибуля

1 large red onion, halved through the stem end, then cut into thin half-moons

1 cup water

½ cup red wine vinegar

1 tablespoon sugar

½ teaspoon salt

1 fresh thyme sprig

If you open my fridge any day of the week, the one thing you'll find there for sure is a jar of beautiful magenta pickled onions. They have a perfect balance of sweetness and acidity and can bring life to any dish. I add them to everything from a traditional Slavic charcuterie platter and pickled herring with potatoes (page 88) to my Golden Beet Vinegret Salad (page 48) and my hearty Crimean Beef Stew with Chickpeas (page 108).

Tightly pack the onion slices into a small, heatproof glass jar with a lid.

In a small saucepan, combine the water, vinegar, salt, sugar, and thyme and bring to a simmer over medium-high heat, stirring to dissolve the sugar. Remove from the heat and pour the brine over the onion. The onion should be completely submerged in the brine. Let cool to room temperature.

Serve the onion slices right away, or cover the jar and store in the refrigerator for up to 2 weeks.

Mom's Famous Spicy and Sour Tomatoes

Мамині мариновані помідори

MAKES ONE 2-QUART JAR
SERVES 8

2 pounds small red tomatoes
(such as Campari or Pearl),
halved lengthwise

1 large green bell pepper, seeded
and roughly chopped

1 medium-size fresh jalapeño chile

4 garlic cloves

1 cup chopped mixed fresh herbs
(such as dill, flat-leaf parsley,
and cilantro)

⅓ cup sunflower or grapeseed oil

⅓ cup distilled white vinegar

2 tablespoons sugar

1 teaspoon salt

These tomatoes are hands down the most popular *zakuska* I serve at my dinners. As you can guess from the name, these are another of my mom's creations. They are very different from traditional pickled tomatoes, which typically call for a vinegary pickling liquid. My mom immerses her tomatoes in a thick, spicy sauce made from fresh herbs, chile, oil, and vinegar. This incredible mixture makes the tomatoes wonderfully refreshing, with a bright pop of acid and a flavor riot of herbs and garlic. I have to warn you, however, that because these might be the most delicious pickled tomatoes you will have ever tasted, it will be hard to wait the three days they need to sit before trying one. I have personally witnessed diners at my pop-ups drinking the leftover pickling liquid once the tomatoes have been wiped out.

Pack the tomato halves into a clean, widemouthed 2-quart glass jar with a tight-fitting lid.

To make the pickling marinade, in a food processor, combine the bell pepper, chile, garlic, herbs, oil, vinegar, sugar, and salt and pulse until a thick, slightly chunky mixture forms, about 30 seconds. Pour the marinade over the tomatoes and screw the lid on the jar.

Refrigerate for at least 3 days before serving. The tomatoes will keep in the refrigerator for up to 1 month. Over time, they will develop even brighter acidity and more complex flavor of slightly fermented tomatoes.

Fermented "Sour" Eggplant

Кислі баклажани

SERVES 5

5 small eggplants (such as Listada de Gandia or Italian), about 1 pound total weight

1 cup sunflower oil, plus more if needed

2 medium carrots, peeled and coarsely grated

1 large yellow onion, chopped

½ medium red bell pepper (2½ ounces), seeded and sliced

1 tablespoon sugar

2 teaspoons salt

1 teaspoon red chile flakes

10 garlic cloves, minced

1 small bunch fresh cilantro, chopped

Growing up in Ukraine, where pickling and fermentation are integral techniques of the culinary culture, I developed a taste for everything fizzy, sour, and funky from a very young age. These "sour" eggplants are one of my grandma Olia's signature dishes, and for me, they are simply irresistible. I could eat countless of these garlicky ferments accompanied by a generous portion of Potato Fried with Pork Belly (page 105) and a thick slice of rye bread. For some reason, fermented eggplants are not as famous as Slavic sour cucumbers, even though they have just as much flavor, if not more.

Preheat the oven to 400°F. Line a large sheet pan with parchment paper.

Place the eggplants on the prepared pan. Bake until soft but not mushy, about 20 minutes. You should be able to pierce them easily with a knife but still feel a tiny bit of resistance. Let cool to room temperature.

In a large frying pan, heat the oil over medium heat. Add the carrots and onion and cook, stirring occasionally, until soft and fragrant, about 10 minutes. Add the bell pepper and cook, stirring occasionally, until the pepper is soft, about 5 more minutes. Season the vegetables with the sugar, salt, and chile flakes and continue to cook, stirring, for 2 more minutes. Transfer the vegetables and oil to a medium bowl and stir in the garlic and cilantro.

To prepare your eggplants for stuffing, cut a lengthwise slit halfway through each eggplant and open the slit like a pocket. Be careful not to cut them all the way through to the bottom; the filling has to remain inside the eggplant pocket.

Generously stuff the eggplants with the filling and place them in a single layer in a wide bowl or a medium-large, deep baking dish. Then pour the oil and vegetable filling remaining in the bowl on top of the stuffed eggplants.

Tightly cover the surface of the eggplants with a piece of plastic wrap and top it with a flat plate or small cutting board. Place something heavy on top. A large jar filled with water works great. You need to weight the eggplants down so they are fully submerged in the oil.

If there is not quite enough oil to cover them, add more as needed. This step is crucial for the fermentation process.

Leave the eggplants in a dark, cool place (no higher than 70°F) for 5 to 7 days. They should get slightly fizzy and taste pleasantly sour. Ferment for a few more days if you want a more robust fermented flavor.

After the fermentation is finished, pack the eggplants with the oil into an airtight container and store in the refrigerator for up to 3 weeks.

Beet and Horseradish Hot Sauce

Хрон з буряком

MAKES ABOUT ¾ CUP

4 ounces horseradish root, peeled and roughly chopped

1 small-to-medium beet, 3½ ounces, peeled and roughly chopped

1½ tablespoons distilled white vinegar, or more to taste

1 teaspoon sugar, or more to taste

½ teaspoon salt, or more to taste

For this fiery, spicy sauce, you'll need to buy fresh horseradish root. Mixed with raw beet, it creates a vivid condiment with a pronounced Slavic flavor profile. I love serving it with rich, fatty meat, such as Pork Shank Braised with Sauerkraut and Beer (page 102), a Slavic charcuterie board, or grilled kielbasa.

In a food processor, combine all the ingredients and pulse until a paste forms. If it looks too dry, add up to ¼ cup water and pulse a few more times. Taste and adjust the seasoning with more vinegar, sugar, or salt if needed.

Use right away, or transfer to an airtight container and refrigerate for up to 3 months.

Lyok

Льок

MAKES ABOUT ¾ CUP

3 garlic cloves, minced

½ cup tightly packed fresh dill leaves

¼ cup tightly packed fresh flat-leaf parsley leaves

2 green onions, white and green parts, coarsely chopped

¼ cup sunflower oil

½ teaspoon freshly ground black pepper

Lyok is the Ukrainian name for a bold mixture of chopped herbs, garlic, and sunflower oil. When added to soups, it imparts a lively burst of flavor and aroma. Add just a tablespoon to a bowl of chicken noodle soup (page 73) or garlicky Georgian chicken (page 92) and you'll taste the difference.

Combine all the ingredients in a food processor and pulse until pureed.

Use right away, or transfer to an airtight container and store in the refrigerator for up to 3 days.

Green Raw Ajika

Зелена аджика

3 medium-size fresh jalapeño chiles

2 large green bell peppers

1 medium shallot

3 garlic cloves

⅓ cup tightly packed fresh cilantro leaves

¼ cup white wine vinegar

1 tablespoon sunflower oil

1 tablespoon sugar

1½ teaspoons salt

The inspiration for this summery sauce comes from Georgia. It calls for a lot of cilantro and green pepper bell, which make it taste particularly refreshing. I love serving it with grilled meat, *chebureki* (page 122), and all kinds of meat dumplings.

Stem, seed, and coarsely chop the chiles and bell peppers. Transfer to a food processor, add the shallot, garlic, cilantro, vinegar, oil, sugar, and salt and pulse until smooth. Taste and adjust the seasoning with salt if needed.

Use right away, or transfer to an airtight container and refrigerate for up to 2 weeks.

Red Ajika

Червона аджика

2 pounds red bell peppers

2 fresh red cayenne chiles

1 large red tomato, about 8 ounces

10 garlic cloves

3 tablespoons apple cider vinegar

1 tablespoon tomato paste

1 tablespoon preserved horseradish

1 tablespoon sugar

1½ teaspoons salt

1 teaspoon ground coriander

½ teaspoon ground cumin

I enjoy making all types of hot sauces, but this *ajika* might be the one I like the best. It has a beautiful aroma of fresh tomatoes and garlic and a very mild spiciness. Unlike green *ajika* (page 168), which is a raw sauce, this one is cooked and will keep in the fridge for a couple of weeks longer.

Stem, seed, and coarsely chop the bell peppers and chiles. Quarter the tomato. Transfer the peppers, chiles, tomato, and garlic to a food processor and pulse until smooth. Add the vinegar, tomato paste, horseradish, sugar, salt, coriander, and cumin and pulse a couple of more times to mix well.

Transfer the mixture to a medium saucepan and bring to a simmer over medium-high heat. Turn down the heat to medium-low and cook the sauce, stirring occasionally, for 15 minutes to blend the flavors. Taste and adjust the seasoning with salt, sugar, or vinegar if needed, then remove from the heat and let cool to room temperature.

Use right away, or store in an airtight container in the refrigerator for up to 1 month.

Horseradish Mayo

Майонез з хроном

MAKES ABOUT 1½ CUPS

1 egg yolk

1 teaspoon Dijon mustard

1 teaspoon white wine vinegar

½ teaspoon salt

¼ teaspoon sugar

¾ cup sunflower oil

1 tablespoon water

¼ cup finely grated fresh horseradish root, or 2 teaspoons preserved horseradish

Despite the fact that this mayo has a spicy kick from the addition of horseradish, it's surprisingly versatile. I use it in my Beet Pickled Deviled Eggs (page 32), on my meat sandwiches, and as a condiment with various Slavic cold cuts.

In a medium bowl, using a large whisk, beat together the egg yolk, mustard, vinegar, salt, and sugar until well blended and smooth. While whisking constantly, begin adding the oil in a very thin, steady stream. Whisk continuously until all the oil is incorporated and the mayo is thick and pale. Then whisk in the water to loosen the texture. Add the horseradish and give the mayo a good stir. Taste and adjust the seasoning with more vinegar, salt, or sugar if needed.

Use right away, or transfer to an airtight container and store in the refrigerator for up to 3 days.

Syr / Tvorog Cheese

Сир

MAKES ABOUT 2 POUNDS (ABOUT 4 CUPS)

4 quarts organic whole milk (not ultra-pasteurized)

1½ cups cultured full-fat buttermilk or kefir

In Ukraine, we call this soft, tangy cheese *syr*. This is sometimes confusing for people who didn't grow up in Ukraine, because in Ukrainian, the word *syr* literally means cheese in general. Ukrainian soft *syr* is exactly the same as Russian *tvorog* and Polish *twaróg*. French *fromage blanc* has a similar flavor and texture, though *syr* is tangier and has a slightly denser texture. *Syr* is used for countless dishes, both sweet and savory. It is a true staple of the Ukrainian kitchen and is one of the most beloved Slavic food products, which is why I have included a recipe for it here.

Pour the milk into a large pot and heat over medium-high heat until it reaches 140°F. Remove from the heat, add the buttermilk, and stir with a large whisk to mix well. Cover the pot and leave it undisturbed at room temperature for 24 to 36 hours. The timing depends on the temperature of your kitchen. The mixture is ready when it has thickened to a yogurt-like consistency.

Place the pot over low heat and begin heating the mixture very slowly (don't bring it to a simmer), gently stirring once or twice with a large, heat-resistant spatula, until the mixture reaches 155°F. This should take about 40 minutes.

As soon as the temperature reaches 155°F, remove the pot from the heat and allow it to sit, undisturbed, until it cools down to room temperature. As the mixture cools, you will see it separate into curds and whey.

Place a large tamis or a colander lined with four layers of extra-fine-weave cheesecloth over a big bowl or pot. Pour the curds and whey into the tamis and allow to drain. When all the visible whey has passed into the bowl, bring the corners of the cheesecloth up to meet and twist them firmly together to squeeze out as much moisture as possible (see Note). Then tie off the twist with kitchen twine. The cheesecloth bundle should resemble a beggar's purse. Leave a loop on the kitchen twine and hang the bundle over your kitchen faucet to allow any remaining whey to drain off for 6 to 8 hours.

Transfer the cheese to an airtight container and store in the refrigerator. It will keep for up to 1 week.

note: Reserve the whey and store it in an airtight container in the refrigerator for up to 2 weeks. Use it in place of milk or water in recipes for bread, blini, and crepes.

Pomegranate Molasses

Гранатова патока

MAKES ABOUT 1 CUP

4 cups 100 percent pomegranate juice (see Note)

½ cup sugar

¼ teaspoon citric acid

note: Be sure to use 100 percent pomegranate juice for this recipe rather than juice made from concentrate. Pom is a good brand.

Ever since I started hosting Georgian pop-up dinners, homemade pomegranate molasses became a pantry staple. It's hard to imagine Georgian Eggplant Rolls (page 29) or beet *pkhali* (page 52) without this tart-sweet sauce.

In a medium saucepan, combine all the ingredients and bring to a boil over medium-high heat. Lower the heat to medium and simmer until the liquid is reduced to about 1 cup and becomes dark and syrupy, 1 to 1½ hours. The color will change from dark purple to garnet. Remove from the heat and let cool slightly, about 10 minutes.

Transfer the molasses to a heatproof glass jar with a lid while it is still warm. As it cools, it will continue to thicken. Cover and store at room temperature or in the refrigerator. It will keep for up to 2 months.

Tart Cranberry and Mint Mors

Морс

**MAKES A GENEROUS
1 QUART; SERVES 6**

8 cups water

10½ ounces cranberries (3 cups)

1 cup tightly packed fresh mint leaves

½ cup sugar

This is the perfect recipe for the cranberry postseason—right after Thanksgiving when grocery stores sell three pounds for a dollar. I never miss those deals and make gallons of cranberry mors for friends and family.

In a medium pot, bring the water to a boil over medium-high heat. Meanwhile, in a food processor, pulse the cranberries until pureed. When the water is boiling, add the pureed cranberries and return to a simmer. Lower the heat to medium-low, add the mint, and simmer for 5 more minutes.

Remove from the heat and let cool slightly. Pour the mint-cranberry mixture through a fine-mesh sieve into a large, heatproof pitcher. Add the sugar and stir until dissolved. Let completely cool before serving.

Serve the drink chilled or over ice. It will keep in an airtight container in the refrigerator for up to 4 days.

Apple-Infused Nastoyanka

Яблучна настоянка

MAKES ABOUT 1 PINT

5 small apples, 12 ounces total weight, peeled

1 whole dried peach, or 2 dried peach halves

2 cups (1 pint) vodka

1 tablespoon honey

note: The apples are edible. They make an excellent boozy sorbet.

Ukrainians mastered the art of vodka infusion centuries ago. Since we have long, cold winters, we use all the berries and other fruits under the sun in an attempt to bottle the spirit of summer. This particular *nastoyanka* is made with small, perfumy apples and a touch of dried peach to deepen the aroma. You can look for small apples at your local farmers' market, or use larger ones and cut them into wedges. Everyone who has tasted this drink has instantly fallen in love with its delicate flavor and intoxicating scent. Serve it chilled before or after a meal.

In a large, widemouthed jar, combine the apples and peach. Pour the vodka over the fruits and add the honey. Stir the mixture with a long spoon until the honey is completely dissolved. Cover the jar with a lid.

Place the jar in a cool, dark place. The infusion will be ready in 1 week. I usually don't strain it, but you can pass it through a fine-mesh sieve lined with a couple of layers of cheesecloth if you like. Serve chilled in shot glasses. It will keep in an airtight container in the refrigerator indefinitely.

Mead

Мед

MAKES 6 CUPS

1 cup raw honey (such as wildflower, acacia, or orange blossom)

5 cups distilled water, at room temperature (70°F)

5 or 6 golden raisins

Centuries ago, mead was a popular alcoholic beverage in what is today Russia, Ukraine, and other areas of northern and Eastern European. But by the Middle Ages, as people started to favor stronger drinks, making mead was almost completely abandoned. Fortunately, it is easy to make this aromatic honey drink. Just get some good-quality raw honey and a few raisins, mix everything with water, and let the natural fermentation do its magic. In less than two weeks, you'll have a delicate alcoholic beverage that will bring joy into your life.

In a widemouthed jar, combine the honey, water, and raisins. Stir until the honey completely dissolves. Cover the jar with a tight-fitting lid and place it in a spot away from direct sunlight.

Stir the contents of the jar vigorously at least twice a day. In a few days, you'll see bubbles starting to form on top of the liquid. That means the fermentation process is going well. Keep the routine going. I usually let my mead ferment for about 10 days. After that, the fermentation process visibly slows down, but you can keep fermenting it for a few more days if you like.

When the mead is ready, transfer it to one or two bottles, cap tightly, and store in the refrigerator for up to 2 months.

Horseradish-Infused Vodka

Хреновуха

MAKES 1½ PINTS

3 ounces fresh horseradish root, peeled and sliced

3 tablespoons buckwheat or other dark honey

2 tablespoons fresh lemon juice

6 cups (1½ pints) vodka

This is probably the most famous Ukrainian vodka-based drink. Known as *khrenovukha*, it's powerful, warming, and pleasantly spicy. It goes exceptionally well with rich, savory dishes, especially during the colder months. Some people claim that *khrenovukha* can cure anything from the flu to a lousy mood. I'm not a doctor, but I think they have a point.

In a large jar, combine the horseradish, honey, lemon juice, and 2 cups of the vodka. Mix well with a long spoon until the honey is completely dissolved. Pour in the remaining 4 cups vodka and cover the jar with a lid.

Place the jar in a cool, dark place, shaking it once a day. The infusion will be ready in 1 week. Strain it through a fine-mesh sieve lined with a couple of layers of cheesecloth, then transfer it to a bottle and cap tightly. Serve chilled in shot glasses. It will keep indefinitely in the refrigerator.

Uzvar

Узвар

MAKES ABOUT 4 QUARTS
SERVES 12

3½ quarts water

1 pound dried fruits (such as apples, pears, prunes, and apricots)

Honey or sugar, for sweetening

We love fruit drinks in Ukraine and enjoy them year-round. This one is a winter version of *kompot* (page 185). It's usually made with prunes, dried apples, and apricots and has a dark amber color and a deeply satisfying flavor.

In a large pot, combine the water and fruits and bring to a boil over medium-high heat. Lower the heat to medium-low and simmer for about 15 minutes. Remove from the heat and let cool for about 30 minutes.

While the mixture is still warm, stir in honey to taste, then let cool completely. You can strain the liquid through a fine-mesh sieve into a pitcher, or you can pour the liquid with the fruits into the pitcher. Refrigerate for at least 1 hour before serving.

Serve the drink chilled. If you decided to keep the fruits in, serve with long dessert spoons for eating the fruits. It will keep in an airtight container in the refrigerator for up to 4 days.

Summer Fruit Kompot

Компот

MAKES ABOUT 3½ QUARTS
SERVES 10 TO 12

3 quarts water

1½ pounds seasonal fruits, stone fruits pitted and cut into chunks if needed and berries and other small fruits left whole

½ cup sugar, plus more if needed

If I had to choose only one drink for the rest of my life, it would be *kompot*. A traditional drink of Eastern Europe, it is made by boiling seasonal fruits with a lot of water and a bit of sugar until you have a super-flavorful and refreshing beverage. I have experimented with mixing all kinds of different fruits together, though my favorite combo is probably stone fruits and berries.

In a large pot, combine the water and fruits and bring to a simmer over medium-high heat. Turn down the heat to medium-low, add the sugar, and mix well with a large spoon to dissolve the sugar. Continue cooking, keeping the liquid slightly below the boiling point at all times, for 15 to 20 minutes. (Keeping the liquid at a simmer helps to save vitamins.) It is ready when the fruits are very soft and the drink tastes good to you.

Remove from the heat and let cool. You can strain the liquid through a fine-mesh sieve into a pitcher, or you can pour the liquid with the fruits into the pitcher. Taste and adjust with more sugar if needed.

Serve the drink chilled or at room temperature. If you decided to keep the fruits in, serve with long dessert spoons for eating the fruits. It will keep in an airtight container in the refrigerator for up to 5 days.

Rhubarb-Strawberry Kisel

Полунично-рененевий кисіль

**MAKES A SCANT 3 QUARTS
SERVES 8 TO 10**

6 ounces rhubarb, trimmed and roughly chopped

6 ounces strawberries, hulled and quartered

2½ quarts plus ½ cup water

½ cup sugar

¼ cup cornstarch

Depending on how much cornstarch you're using, *kisel* can be a thick drink or a light dessert you can eat with a spoon. Both ways are delicious and remind me of my early childhood when I would have *kisel* and cookies as a snack before a late-afternoon nap. That was the only way my grandma could trick me into going to sleep in the middle of the day.

In a medium pot, combine the rhubarb, strawberries, and 2½ quarts of the water and bring to a boil over medium-high heat. Lower the heat to medium and cook, keeping the mixture just below a boil and stirring occasionally, until the rhubarb and strawberries are very soft, about 15 minutes. Add the sugar, mix well with a spoon, and continue cooking until the sugar dissolves, about 1 minute longer.

Meanwhile, in a small bowl, mix together the cornstarch and the remaining ½ cup water to make a slurry. Using a large whisk, stir the slurry into the rhubarb-strawberry mixture and continue to cook until the mixture thickens slightly, about 5 minutes longer. Remove from the heat and let cool to room temperature.

Serve the drink chilled or at room temperature with long dessert spoons for eating the rhubarb and berries. It will keep in an airtight container in the refrigerator for up to 5 days.

DESSERTS

✦ ✦ ✦
✦ ✦
✦

ДЕСЕРТИ

EASTERN EUROPEANS DON'T typically eat dessert every day. Sweets are more of a special occasion treat served with tea when guests come by or during feasts and celebrations. In Ukraine, home cooks especially like to make all sorts of cakes, pies, and sweet pastries filled with fresh fruits or jams, with recipes varying from region to region.

Growing up in the south, I indulged in local sunflower seed halva packaged in humongous bricks and sliced to order. I also loved the thick apple marmalade called *povydlo*, which my grandma would buy for making rugelach and oven-baked *pyrizhky*. My mom is also a serious baker, but unlike my grandma, she is more into cakes and pies. I love to flip through her old recipe notebooks in search of some forgotten culinary treasures, like the Karpatka Cake on page 207.

In western Ukraine, both desserts and cafés are generally more classy and elegant than in other regions. This is especially true in the city of Lviv, an architectural and cultural gem that is home to many small, charming old-style European cafeterias that sell Hungarian strudel with dozens of different fillings. Local pastry shops serve tiny cups of Viennese coffee with slices of splendid layered cakes, Lviv cheesecake, and delicious handcrafted chocolate.

Lviv is indeed a heaven for dessert lovers. But no matter what part of the country you're visiting, iconic desserts like honey cake and *beze* (caramel-topped meringue) can be found in almost any restaurant or bakery—or you can make them at home following the recipes in this chapter.

Berry Sorbet

Ягідний сорбет

SERVES 6 TO 8

½ cup granulated sugar

½ cup water

2 cups strawberries, hulled

1 cup blueberries

1 cup blackberries

¼ cup fresh lemon juice

This sorbet is one of the most nostalgic dishes in this book and is probably my earliest food memory. When I was a toddler, my grandpa often took me with him to his friend's car repair shop to spend the whole afternoon. Halfway there, we always stopped at the local café to eat this wonderful berry dessert. It was such a treat! I have tried to re-create what I remember from those days, making this sorbet berry-forward, refreshing, and with a hint of tartness.

In a small saucepan, combine the sugar and water and bring to a boil over medium-high heat, stirring to dissolve the sugar. Simmer until syrupy, about 2 minutes, then remove from the heat and let the syrup cool to room temperature.

Combine all the berries in a blender and puree until smooth. Add the syrup and lemon juice and blend on low speed for a few seconds to bring everything together.

Pour the mixture into an ice cream maker and churn according to the manufacturer's instructions, for about 30 minutes. It should be smooth and have the consistency of soft serve. The timing will vary according to the maker; mine churns a batch in about 30 minutes.

Transfer the sorbet to a freezer-safe container and freeze for a couple of hours until firm before serving. It will keep in the freezer for up to 2 weeks.

Remove the sorbet from the freezer about 15 minutes before serving to allow it to soften a bit. Then scoop it into serving bowls and serve immediately.

Sour Cream Ice Cream

with Sea Buckthorn Sauce

Сметанкове морозиво з обліпиховим сиропом

SERVES 4 TO 6

FOR THE ICE CREAM

16 ounces sour cream (2 cups)

3 egg yolks

½ cup plus 1 tablespoon sugar

1 tablespoon pure vanilla extract

¼ teaspoon salt

FOR THE SAUCE

½ cup sea buckthorn berries (fresh or frozen)

2 tablespoons sugar

I found this recipe in a nineteenth-century Ukrainian cookbook. It makes a luscious sour cream ice cream that is delicious on its own but is also extremely good drizzled with a bright orange sauce made from sea buckthorn berries. The berries are popular in Russia, Ukraine, Scandinavia, and other cold climates where the sea buckthorn shrub thrives. You can find these tart berries in the freezer section of your local Russian store or online. They also make killer quick preserves and robust fruit tea full of vitamins and antioxidants.

In a large bowl, whisk together the sour cream, egg yolks, sugar, vanilla, and salt until blended. Pour the sour cream mixture into a medium saucepan and heat over medium-low heat, stirring constantly with the whisk, until thickened, 7 to 10 minutes. The mixture should be the consistency of a slightly loose custard.

Remove from the heat and pour into a heatproof medium bowl. Cover with plastic wrap, pressing it directly against the mixture to prevent a skin from forming. Let cool to room temperature, then refrigerate for at least 2 hours or preferably overnight.

Meanwhile, make the sauce. In a small saucepan, combine the berries and sugar and bring to a simmer over medium-high heat. Continue simmering, stirring occasionally, until the mixture thickens slightly, 3 to 5 minutes. Remove from the heat and let cool to room temperature. Then transfer to an airtight container and refrigerate until needed.

Pour the chilled ice cream base into an ice cream maker and churn according to the manufacturer's instructions. It should have the consistency of soft serve. The timing will vary according to the maker; mine churns a batch in 35 to 40 minutes.

Transfer the ice cream to a freezer-safe container and freeze for a few hours until firm. It will keep in the freezer for up to 1 week.

Remove the ice cream from the freezer 10 to 15 minutes before serving to allow it to soften a bit. Scoop the ice cream into serving bowls, top with the sauce, and serve.

Sunflower Seed Halva

Халва з соняшнику

SERVES 6 TO 8

14 ounces shelled sunflower seeds (about 3 cups)

½ teaspoon salt

1 egg white, at room temperature

1 cup sugar

¼ cup water

1 teaspoon pure vanilla extract

Native to the New World, the sunflower was introduced in Ukraine in the early eighteenth century, but for more than a hundred years, it was appreciated only for its beautiful and exotic flowers. It was only in the nineteenth century that it became an important agricultural crop, prized for its oil production. Today, Ukraine is a land of endless sunflower fields and is one of the world's leading exporters of sunflower oil. Ukrainians use the oil in their daily cooking and dried sunflower seeds as an everyday snack. No wonder sunflower seed halva is so popular there. Store-bought halva has always been a tad too sweet for me, so I prefer to make my own less sweet version.

In a dry large frying pan, toast the sunflower seeds over medium-high heat until lightly golden, about 7 minutes. Shake the pan frequently to make sure the seeds are toasting evenly.

Remove the pan from the heat, pour the seeds into a food processor, and let cool down slightly. Process the seeds until a smooth paste forms, then add the salt and process briefly to mix well. (If your food processor is small, process them in a couple of batches.) Transfer the sunflower seed paste to a medium bowl and set aside.

Line an 8-inch square baking dish with two pieces of parchment paper. They should cover the bottom and overlap all four sides by a couple of inches.

In a stand mixer fitted with the whisk attachment, whip the egg white on medium speed until it holds soft peaks. Turn off the mixer and leave the egg white in the bowl.

In a small saucepan, mix together the sugar and water and bring to a simmer over medium-high heat, stirring with a heat-resistant spatula until the sugar dissolves. Then simmer the sugar without stirring until the syrup registers 235°F on a candy thermometer (soft-ball stage). Remove from the heat.

With the mixer on medium-high speed, add the vanilla to the whipped egg white, then start slowly pouring in the syrup. Continue whipping until all the syrup has been added and the mixture becomes thick, glossy, and falls in a wide ribbon when the whisk is lifted.

Add the egg white to the sunflower seed paste and quickly mix with a rubber spatula until the mixture is smooth and uniform. Do not overmix. Transfer the mixture to the prepared dish and smooth the surface with the spatula.

Let the halva set at room temperature for at least 1 hour. Using the parchment overhang, lift the halva out of the dish and transfer it to a cutting board. Cut the halva into squares and serve. It will keep in an airtight container at room temperature for up to 10 days.

Baked Apples

with Tvorog Cheese

Печені яблука

SERVES 4

4 medium Granny Smith or other crisp, hard apples

⅔ cup tvorog cheese (about 7 ounces), homemade (page 174) or store-bought

1 tablespoon raisins

1 tablespoon light and floral honey, plus more for serving

1 tablespoon pine nuts

¼ teaspoon ground cinnamon

1 ounce fresh red currants (optional)

Making these lovely baked apples stuffed with cheese and pine nuts is one of my favorite ways to celebrate fall and its generous harvest season. They are warm and comforting, and work great as a healthier dessert option, especially for kids. They also make a wonderful breakfast alongside a cup of freshly brewed coffee. If you don't have any Ukrainian cheese on hand, French *fromage blanc* makes a good substitute.

Preheat the oven to 350°F. Line a small sheet pan with parchment paper.

Using a sharp, small knife, slice off the stem end of each apple. Carve out the core with the seeds, being careful not to cut all the way through to the bottom. You want the apple to hold the stuffing like a small bowl.

In a small bowl, combine the cheese, raisins, and honey and mix well with a spoon. Stuff each apple with an equal amount of the cheese mixture and top with the pine nuts, cinnamon, and currants (if using), dividing them evenly.

Arrange the apples on the prepared sheet pan. Bake the apples until they are soft but not mushy when pierced with a knife, 30 to 35 minutes. Remove from the oven and let cool until warm.

Serve the apples slightly warm drizzled with a little honey.

Vyshyvanka Bars

Пиріг "Вишиванка"

SERVES 8

4 cups all-purpose flour, plus more for dusting

½ teaspoon baking powder

½ teaspoon salt

1 cup cold unsalted butter, cubed

2 eggs

¼ cup sugar

1 cup plus 2 tablespoons (12 ounces) tart jam (such as plum, black currant, or cranberry)

Despite being possibly the simplest of all Slavic pastries, these bars are unbelievably satisfying. In Ukraine, we call this sweet *vyshyvanka*, after our traditional embroidered shirt because the top resembles the pattern on the shirt. It was the first baked dessert I ever made as a kid, and I have loved it dearly ever since. To make this dessert shine, you need to use a tart jam. My personal favorite is plum, but black currant and cranberry work great as well.

In a food processor, combine the flour, baking powder, and salt and pulse briefly two or three times to mix. Scatter the butter over the flour mixture and pulse a few times until the butter and flour are well incorporated and the butter pieces are about the size of peas. Transfer the mixture to a large bowl and add the eggs and sugar. Mix all the ingredients together with a rubber spatula until the dough comes together in a shaggy mass. Then begin kneading the dough with your hands in the bowl until you have a smooth ball. The dough will be soft and slightly sticky. Work very quickly or the butter will start melting from the warmth of your hands.

Transfer the dough to a cutting board and cut off a good chunk, about one-third of the total weight. Wrap it tightly in plastic wrap and put it into the freezer for 1 hour. Wrap the remaining two-thirds of the dough in plastic wrap and refrigerate it for 1 hour.

Preheat the oven to 350°F.

Cut a 12-by-15-inch sheet of parchment paper. Remove the larger piece of dough from the refrigerator, place it on the parchment, and roll it out into a rectangle ½ inch thick. Transfer the parchment paper together with the dough to a large sheet pan. Evenly spread the jam over the dough.

Remove the smaller piece of dough from the freezer and, using the large holes on a box grater, grate the dough evenly over the jam.

Bake the pastry until the top is lightly golden, 30 to 35 minutes. Let completely cool on the pan on a wire rack, then slice and serve.

Ukrainian Cheesecake

with Apricots

Сирник з абрикосами

SERVES 8

1 pound tvorog cheese, homemade (page 174) or store-bought

¼ cup sour cream

2 eggs

2 teaspoons pure vanilla extract

¼ cup sugar, plus more for topping

¼ teaspoon salt

3 tablespoons semolina

Nonstick cooking spray, for the baking dish

5 medium apricots, halved and pitted

Almost every country has a favorite cheese-based dessert. Ukraine is no exception. We make ours with tangy *syr* cheese and often add fresh or dried fruits, berries, or, in my case, fresh apricots. This cheesecake is very filling, and I prefer to eat it for breakfast with a cup of freshly brewed coffee or tea. It just makes my morning so much better.

Preheat the oven to 350°F.

In a food processor, combine the cheese, sour cream, eggs, vanilla, sugar, and salt. Process until the cheese mixture is smooth and uniform, about 1 minute. Transfer it to a medium bowl and, using a rubber spatula, gently mix in the semolina.

Spray an 8-inch square baking dish with cooking spray. Transfer the cheese mixture to the prepared dish. Using the spatula or a spoon, smooth it into an even layer. Arrange the apricot halves, cut side up, on top, and evenly sprinkle them with a generous pinch of sugar.

Bake the cheesecake until the edges are golden brown and the center is no longer jiggly, 45 to 55 minutes. Turn the oven off and open the oven door halfway. Let the cheesecake sit in the oven for about 40 minutes as the oven cools down, then remove it from the oven and let cool completely.

Serve the cheesecake at room temperature. It will keep, covered with plastic wrap, in the refrigerator for up to 4 days.

Beze

with Peanuts and Honey Caramel

Безе з арахісом і медовою карамеллю

FOR THE MERINGUE

3 egg whites

1 teaspoon pure vanilla extract

¼ teaspoon salt

¼ teaspoon cream of tartar

¾ cup sugar

1½ tablespoons cornstarch

½ cup unsalted dry-roasted peanuts, roughly chopped

FOR THE HONEY CARAMEL

4 tablespoons unsalted butter

⅓ cup light and floral honey (such as clover or orange blossom)

1 tablespoon buckwheat honey (optional)

1 cup heavy cream

¼ teaspoon salt

Unsalted dry-roasted peanuts, roughly chopped, for topping

This caramel-topped meringue is another iconic Soviet dessert. For me, *beze* was always hit or miss because the version sold in our local pastry shop was often too dry and had very little caramel. I made sure this one will be nothing like that. My *beze* has a crispy shell but is still perfectly soft and chewy inside. I top it with the loveliest honey caramel, which is so good I can barely stop myself from eating the whole batch before the *beze* is ready. I use a little bit of Ukrainian dark buckwheat honey to intensify the flavor of the caramel, but this is totally optional.

Preheat the oven to 265°F. Line a sheet pan with parchment paper.

To make the meringue, in a stand mixer fitted with the whisk attachment, whip together the egg whites, vanilla, and salt on medium-low speed until the egg whites are light, frothy, and hold soft peaks. Increase the speed to medium and add the cream of tartar. Then start adding the sugar in a slow, steady stream. When all the sugar has been added, increase the speed to medium-high and continue whipping until the meringue is stiff and glossy. Using a rubber spatula, gently fold in the cornstarch and peanuts just until evenly distributed.

Using a large serving spoon, scoop the meringue in four equal portions onto the prepared sheet pan, spacing them about 2 inches apart. Each one should be slightly larger than a baseball. Bake the meringues until they are completely dry outside and can be easily lifted from the parchment, 50 to 60 minutes. They should have barely any color. Transfer the sheet pan to a wire rack and let the meringues cool completely and dry out for at least a few hours or even up to overnight. Peel the meringues off the parchment when ready to serve.

Meanwhile, make the honey caramel. In a medium saucepan, melt together the butter and both honeys over medium-high heat. Bring to a simmer and cook without stirring until the mixture turns deep amber, 6 to 7 minutes. Add the cream and salt. The mixture will bubble vigorously, but that's normal. Mix the caramel sauce with a small whisk until it comes together and then remove the pan from the heat. Let the sauce cool for 10 to 15 minutes.

Pour the sauce into a jar and let cool to room temperature. Cover tightly and refrigerate for at least 3 hours or preferably overnight. The caramel sauce might appear too liquidy when you pour it into the jar, but it will thicken after a few hours in the refrigerator.

To serve, place the meringues on four dessert plates, drizzle them with the sauce, and top with a scattering of peanuts.

Cream Horns
with Swiss Meringue Buttercream
Трубочки з кремом

SERVES 8

FOR THE PASTRY HORNS

1 tablespoon all-purpose flour

1 large or 2 smaller puff pastry sheets (preferably all butter), about 8 ounces total weight, thawed if frozen

Nonstick cooking spray, for the molds

1 egg

1 tablespoon water

FOR THE SWISS MERINGUE BUTTERCREAM

3 egg whites, at room temperature

1 cup granulated sugar

1 cup unsalted butter, cubed and at room temperature

2 teaspoons pure vanilla extract

Confectioners' sugar, for serving

note: I use cream horn molds about 4½ inches long and 1½ inches wide at the broad end. You can find them in well-stocked cookware stores or online.

Everyone who was a kid during the Soviet period knows these cream horns, which are called *trubochki*. When I was little, every bakery, cafeteria, and grocery store in Ukraine sold them. People fell mostly into two categories, those who liked meringue filling and those who preferred buttercream. I could never choose which one I liked more, so I decided to combine them into the light, delicious Swiss meringue buttercream used here.

Preheat the oven to 375°F. Line a large sheet pan with parchment paper.

To make the pastry horns, lightly dust a work surface with the flour. Gently roll out the puff pastry into a rectangle about 15 inches long, 12 inches wide, and ⅛ inch thick. Using a ruler and a pastry cutter, cut the dough into ten 1½-by-12-inch strips. (If you are using two pastry sheets, roll out each sheet 12 inches long, ⅛ inch thick, and wide enough to yield five 1½-by-12-inch strips.)

Spray ten cream horn molds (see Note) with cooking spray. Starting from the pointed end, wrap a strip of dough over the outside of a mold, slightly overlapping it as you go. Lightly brush the end of the strip with water and seal securely at the top. Repeat with the remaining dough strips and prepared molds.

Arrange the wrapped molds on the prepared sheet pan, spacing them about 2 inches apart. The pastries will get larger as they bake, so they need to be well spaced. In a small bowl, whisk together the egg and water with a fork. Lightly brush each pastry with the egg wash, then send the pan to the oven. Bake the pastries until puffy, crispy, and lightly golden, 20 to 22 minutes. Transfer the pastries to a wire rack and let cool for 10 minutes. Carefully remove the pastry cones from the molds while they are still warm and then let cool completely on the rack.

While the pastry cones are baking and cooling, make the buttercream. Pour water to a depth of about 3 inches into a medium pot and bring to a boil over medium-high heat.

In a stand mixer fitted with the whisk attachment, whip together the egg whites and granulated sugar on medium-low speed until the mixture is slightly frothy. Place the bowl over the pot of boiling water and stir constantly with a whisk until the mixture reaches 160°F and the sugar has dissolved.

Return the bowl to the mixer stand and begin whipping on medium speed, gradually increasing the speed to medium-high. Continue to whip until the meringue is fluffy, glossy, and holds stiff peaks, 5 to 10 minutes. The mixture needs to cool to room temperature (68° to 70°F). If it feels too warm, just wait for a few minutes before continuing. Switch to the paddle attachment, turn down the speed to medium-low, and start adding the butter, a cube at a time. Make sure each addition is fully incorporated before adding another cube. When all the butter has been added, add the vanilla and continue to beat on medium-low speed until well blended and smooth.

Transfer the buttercream to a large piping bag fitted with a large star tip. Pipe the buttercream into the cooled pastry cones, filling each one generously.

When ready to serve, dust the cream horns with confectioners' sugar. Leftover cream horns will keep in an airtight container at room temperature for up to 3 days.

Karpatka Cake

Торт "Карпатка"

SERVES 8

FOR THE FROSTING

2 cups whole milk

2 eggs

⅔ cup granulated sugar

¼ cup cornstarch

2 teaspoons pure vanilla extract

¼ teaspoon salt

2 tablespoons orange liqueur

Finely grated zest of 1 orange

¾ cup unsalted butter, at room temperature

FOR THE PÂTE À CHOUX

⅓ cup whole milk

⅓ cup water

6 tablespoons unsalted butter

½ teaspoon salt

¼ teaspoon granulated sugar

¾ cup all-purpose flour

3 eggs

Sunflower or other neutral oil, for oiling the spatula

Confectioners' sugar, for dusting

I found this cake recipe in my mom's old Soviet-era notebook. Somebody gave it to her decades ago, and she had completely forgotten about it. I decided to use it in this book, but only after adding my own little spin: a dash of bright orange liqueur and some aromatic grated orange zest. Imagine the largest, most decadent éclair you can conjure, and that's what Karpatka cake is. It is like a rich cloud of milky frosting trapped between two layers of *pâte à choux*. (The name translates to Carpathian cake, so-called because the sugar-dusted craggy-topped pastry recalls the snow-capped peaks of the Carpathian Mountains.) It can also be a dangerous dessert, because once you've tasted it, it's difficult not to eat the rest of the cake in one sitting.

To make the frosting, in a medium saucepan, heat the milk to 180°F. While the milk is heating, in a medium-large bowl, whisk together the eggs, granulated sugar, cornstarch, vanilla, and salt until well blended. Carefully pour about half of the hot milk into the egg mixture while stirring constantly. Then slowly pour the egg mixture into the saucepan, stirring as you do, and cook over medium-low heat, stirring constantly with the whisk so the mixture doesn't scorch on the bottom.

Heat the custard until it comes to a simmer and thickens, stirring constantly. It should have a pudding-like consistency and coat the back of a spoon. This should take about 5 minutes. Remove the custard from the heat and pour it into a heatproof container. Whisk in the orange liqueur and orange zest. Cover with a piece of plastic wrap, pressing it directly onto the surface to prevent a skin from forming. Set aside and let cool to room temperature.

Meanwhile, make the pâte à choux. Preheat the oven to 375°F. Cover the bottom and sides of two 8-inch springform pans with parchment paper.

In a medium, heavy saucepan, combine the milk, water, butter, salt, and granulated sugar and bring to a boil over medium-high heat. As soon as the mixture boils, add the flour and start stirring vigorously with a wooden spoon until a tight dough forms and pulls away from the sides of the pan, about 2 minutes. When you see a skin of dough forming on the bottom of the pan, remove the pan from the heat.

Let the dough cool for a few minutes, then add the eggs, one at a time, beating well after each addition with the wooden spoon until fully incorporated before adding the next egg. When all the eggs have been incorporated, you should have a glossy, thick, sticky batter.

Divide the batter evenly between the prepared springform pans, then spread the batter in each pan with an oiled rubber spatula. The surface doesn't have to be too smooth. Transfer both pans to the oven and bake the pastry until golden, 25 to 35 minutes. Let cool completely in the pans on wire racks.

To finish the frosting, in a stand mixer fitted with the whisk attachment, whip the butter on medium-high speed until pale and fluffy, 3 to 4 minutes. Turn down the speed to low and start adding the cooled custard, 1 tablespoon at a time. Make sure each addition is fully incorporated with the butter before adding another spoonful. When all the custard has been incorporated, the frosting should be the consistency of whipped cream.

To assemble the cake, unclasp and lift off the sides from each springform pan. Then, using a wide spatula, carefully lift the layers from the pan bottoms. Reassemble one of the pans (make sure it is at room temperature), clasping the sides in place. Choose the flatter of the two layers and place it on the bottom of the reassembled pan. Top the layer with the frosting, smoothing it with a rubber spatula. Gently set the second layer on the frosting. Cover the pan with plastic wrap and refrigerate the cake until the frosting is firm and fully set, about 3 hours.

When ready to serve, unclasp and carefully lift off the pan sides. Using a long, wide metal spatula, carefully lift the cake from the pan bottom and transfer it to a serving platter. Dust the cake with confectioners' sugar and slice it into serving pieces. Serve right away. Leftover cake will keep in the refrigerator for up to 2 days.

Glorious Honey Cake

Торт "Медовик"

SERVES 8

FOR THE CAKE LAYERS

½ cup light and floral honey (such as clover or wildflower)

½ cup unsalted butter

½ cup sugar

3 eggs

3¾ cups all-purpose flour, plus more for dusting

1½ teaspoons baking soda

¼ teaspoon salt

FOR THE FROSTING

1 cup heavy cream, cold

1 cup plus 2 tablespoons sugar

1 teaspoon pure vanilla extract

1¼ pounds sour cream, at room temperature (2½ cups)

½ cup chopped toasted walnuts, for decorating

I got this recipe from my good friend Halia, a San Francisco Bay Area resident who is from Ukraine. She is an incredibly gifted baker and a perfect partner in crime for all sorts of culinary projects. When I tasted her amazing honey cake for the first time, it felt like a revelation. I asked her to join my pop-ups as a pastry chef, and since then, this honey cake has been our signature dessert. Our guests love it so much that they will probably never let us take it off the menu.

To make the cake layers, in a medium saucepan, melt together the honey, butter, and sugar over medium heat, stirring with a heat-resistant spatula until the mixture is well mixed, about 4 minutes.

Transfer the honey mixture to a large bowl and let sit for a few minutes until warm to the touch but not hot. Add the eggs and whisk vigorously until the mixture is smooth and the eggs are fully incorporated.

In a medium bowl, stir together the flour, baking soda, and salt. Using the spatula, gradually fold the flour mixture into the honey-egg mixture. The dough should be very soft and barely sticky. If the dough is too sticky, fold in a couple more tablespoons of flour. Shape the dough into a ball, wrap in plastic wrap, and refrigerate for 1 hour.

Preheat the oven to 400°F. Line two large sheet pans with parchment paper.

Unwrap the dough and place it on a lightly floured work surface. Divide the dough into ten equal pieces. Set aside nine pieces, keeping them covered with a kitchen towel. Roll out the remaining piece into a round about ⅛ inch thick. Using a 9-inch plate as a template, invert it onto the dough round and trace around the edge with a small knife. Lift off the plate and pull away and reserve the dough scraps. Carefully transfer the dough round to a prepared sheet pan. Roll out and trim a second dough piece the same way. Transfer it to the same sheet pan.

Bake the layers until they turn deep golden brown, 5 to 7 minutes. Transfer them to a wire rack and let cool completely. While the layers are baking, ready two more layers, place them on the second prepared pan, and slip them into the oven as soon as the first two layers are removed. Repeat until all of the dough pieces are rolled out and baked, always reserving the dough scraps.

When all ten layers are baked, spread all the reserved dough scraps on one of the sheet pans and bake until crispy and golden brown, 5 to 7 minutes. Let cool on the pan on a wire rack to room temperature.

While the dough scraps are cooling, make the frosting. In a medium bowl, using an electric mixer, whip together the cream, sugar, and vanilla on medium speed until stiff peaks form. Using a rubber spatula, carefully fold in the sour cream just until incorporated.

Transfer the cooled dough scraps to a food processor, add the walnuts, and pulse briefly until the texture of fine crumbs.

To assemble the cake, place a cake layer on a flat serving platter and top it with a few tablespoons of the frosting. Using an offset spatula, evenly spread the frosting to cover the layer evenly. Top with a second cake layer and spread with frosting the same way. Continue to stack the cake layers and spread them with frosting until there are no cake layers left. Evenly spread the remaining frosting over the top and sides of the cake. Sprinkle the cake crumb–walnut mixture evenly on top.

Cover and refrigerate the cake for at least 4 hours or preferably overnight before serving.

Cranberry-Walnut Strudel

Штрудель з журавлиною та горіхами

SERVES 6

FOR THE FILLING

12 ounces fresh or thawed frozen cranberries (about 3¼ cups)

1 cup granulated sugar

1 orange zest strip, 2 inches long

1 cinnamon stick

½ cup chopped toasted walnuts

FOR THE DOUGH

1½ cups plus 1 tablespoon all-purpose flour, plus more for dusting

1 egg

½ cup lukewarm water (110° to 115°F)

5½ tablespoons unsalted butter, melted and cooled, plus more for the bowl

¼ teaspoon salt

1 tablespoon confectioners' sugar, for serving

Whipped cream or Sour Cream Ice Cream (page 192; without the sauce), for serving

At one point in history, a part of western Ukraine was under Hungarian rule. This delightful pastry is reminiscent of those times. In the city of Lviv, an important cultural center of the region, there is a whole restaurant dedicated to strudel. It offers countless fillings, both sweet and savory. My favorite is cranberry with a handful of walnuts. I love making strudel in early December when there are plenty of cranberries left from Thanksgiving.

To make the filling, in a medium saucepan, combine 9 ounces (2½ cups) of the cranberries, the granulated sugar, orange zest, and cinnamon stick and bring to a boil over medium-high heat. Lower the heat to medium and simmer the mixture until it thickens and most of the berries have split and broken down, 8 to 10 minutes. Add the remaining 3 ounces (¾ cup) cranberries and cook for a few more minutes until they soften. Remove the saucepan from the heat. Remove and discard the orange zest and cinnamon stick and let the filling cool completely. (The filling can be made up to 3 days in advance and stored in an airtight container in the refrigerator.)

To make the dough, in a stand mixer fitted with the paddle attachment, combine the flour, egg, water, 2 tablespoons of the butter, and the salt. Mix on low speed until the dough starts to come together, about 1 minute. Then switch to the dough hook and knead on medium-low speed until the dough is completely smooth and elastic, 5 to 7 minutes. Lightly brush a medium bowl with melted butter and transfer the dough to the bowl. Cover the bowl with plastic wrap and let the dough rest in a warm place (70° to 80°F) for 40 minutes. It should become very soft and stretchy.

Preheat the oven to 375°F.

Transfer the dough to a lightly floured work surface. Roll it out it into a round ¼ inch thick. Then slide your hands under the dough so it rests on the backs of your hands and start gently stretching it with your knuckles, working from the center to the edges and at the same time rotating the dough to ensure you are stretching the entire round evenly. This is just like stretching the crust for a homemade pizza.

When the dough is too large to handle with your knuckles, lay a tablecloth on the work surface, generously dust the tablecloth with flour, and lay the dough on the tablecloth. Now, using your hands and working from all sides, stretch the dough as thinly as you can into a large rectangle. Try not to create any holes. If the dough rips, just pinch it together to seal the hole. The dough should be so thin that you can easily see your hand through it. Using kitchen shears or a pastry or pizza cutter, cut off all the uneven edges. The rectangle should be about 18 by 20 inches.

Move the tablecloth so a short side of the rectangle is facing you. Spread the cooled cranberry filling on the half of the dough closest to you, leaving a roughly 2-inch border uncovered on all sides. Sprinkle the filling evenly with the walnuts. Lightly brush the other half of the dough with some of the remaining butter.

Fold the 2-inch border at bottom half over the filling, then fold in the sides. Using the tablecloth to lift and guide the dough, roll the dough away from you all the way to the end. Then gently move the strudel, seam side down, onto a sheet of parchment paper. Place the parchment with the strudel on a sheet pan, then brush the strudel with the remaining butter.

Bake the strudel until golden, 40 to 50 minutes. Remove from the oven and let cool on the pan on a wire rack for 15 minutes.

Sprinkle the warm strudel with the confectioners' sugar. Cut into thick slices and serve warm topped with the whipped cream or with a scoop of ice cream on the side.

Izba Cake

Торт "Смерекова Хата"

SERVES 6 TO 8

FOR THE DOUGH

3 cups all-purpose flour, plus more for dusting

1 cup sour cream

¾ cup plus 2 tablespoons cold butter, cubed

½ teaspoon salt

FOR THE FILLING

1¾ pounds frozen dark cherries, thawed

⅓ cup granulated sugar

1 teaspoon fresh lemon juice

FOR THE FROSTING

3½ cups sour cream (1¾ pounds)

1⅔ cups confectioners' sugar

1 tablespoon pure vanilla extract

1 ounce dark chocolate, finely grated, for dusting

Although this is one of the lesser known of the many Eastern European desserts, it is especially delicious. After the collapse of the Soviet Union, this cake fell out of fashion, but I think it could make a splendid comeback. I love its simple sour cream frosting and delightful cherry filling. It is both a bit time-consuming to make and very straightforward. If you're looking for a fun cooking project to make with your kids, look no further. The word *izba* refers to a traditional A-frame Slavic wood hut, which your finished cake will resemble.

To make the dough, lightly dust a cutting board. In a food processor, combine the flour, sour cream, butter, and salt and pulse briefly about eight times until the dough comes together in a rough mass. Transfer the dough to a lightly floured work surface and, working quickly, bring the dough together with your hands and form it into a rectangle. Divide the rectangle into five equal pieces, each weighing 5½ ounces, and shape each piece into a small rectangle. Arrange the rectangles in a single layer on the prepared cutting board, cover with plastic wrap, and refrigerate for 1 hour.

While the dough chills, make the filling. In a medium saucepan, combine the cherries, granulated sugar, and lemon juice and bring to a simmer over medium-high heat. Cook, stirring with a heat-resistant spatula, until the mixture is slightly syrupy and the cherries still hold their shape, 3 to 5 minutes. Remove from the heat, let cool completely, then pour the filling into a fine-mesh sieve placed over a bowl, draining the cherries well. Reserve the juice for another use and set the cherries aside until needed.

Position two racks in the center of the oven and preheat the oven to 425°F. Line three sheet pans (9 by 13 inches) with parchment paper.

Lightly dust the work surface with flour. The dough is very delicate and should stay cold as long as possible, so work with one piece at a time and keep the others refrigerated. Remove one piece of the dough from the refrigerator and roll it out into a large, thin rectangle. Using a ruler and a pastry cutter, trim the edges to a neat 9-by-10-inch rectangle. Cut the rectangle into three 3-by-10-inch strips.

Arrange ten or eleven cherries in a single line down the center of each strip, then fold the dough over the cherries to form a long, straight tube. Pinch together the seams and ends to seal. Place the tubes, seam side down, on one of the prepared pans. Repeat with the remaining four dough pieces and cherries to make fifteen tubes in all, dividing the tubes evenly among the three pans and spacing them evenly apart on the pans. Poke the top of each tube with a toothpick about five times, spacing the holes evenly along the length. This will allow steam to escape.

Place two pans on the top middle rack and the third pan on the lower middle rack. Bake the tubes, switching the pans between the racks and rotating them back to front about halfway through baking, for 20 minutes. The tubes should barely take on color. Let cool completely on the pans on wire racks.

While the tubes are cooling, make the frosting, put the sour cream into a large bowl. Add the confectioners' sugar and vanilla and stir to mix, then whip with an electric mixer on medium-high speed until light and frothy, 3 to 5 minutes. Cover and refrigerate until needed.

Once the cherry tubes are completely cooled inside and outside, trim the ends with a knife to make them all exactly the same length. Spread a few tablespoons of the frosting on a large platter and arrange five cherry tubes side by side on top. Cover the tubes with a generous amount of frosting, then top with four tubes side by side, centering them on the five tubes, and cover with a generous amount of frosting. Repeat to make three more levels, one with three tubes, one with two tubes, and the final one with one tube, spreading each level with frosting. The assembled cake will have an A-frame shape resembling a traditional hut. Cover the sides of the cake with the remaining frosting.

Cover and refrigerate the cake for at least 6 hours or preferably overnight. Just before serving, dust with the chocolate.

Acknowledgments

To my Ukrainian family, especially my mom and grandma, who are phenomenal cooks, marvelous hostesses, and the most adventurous eaters I've ever met. I'm glad that I can always come to you for words of wisdom, culinary advice, and unique recipes. You taught me that food should bring people together, give them joy, comfort, and a sense of belonging. I'm forever grateful for our loud bountiful feasts and quiet family dinners, and I know that we have many more to come.

I'd like to thank my agent Leslie Jonath who's not only one of the kindest and most thoughtful people I know but also an exceptional professional. Leslie is my rock and shield, and she is the reason this cookbook writing journey was so easy and enjoyable for me. I already can't wait for our next adventure together. I wish that every author could find their own Leslie.

To Debbie Berne who designed this book and made it so elegant and beautiful. I dreamed of *Budmo!* for years, and Debbie not only brought it to life but navigated me through the whole process. I'm most grateful to her for grasping my vision and concept even before I could form them into words.

To my copy editor Sharon Silva who was infinitely patient with me, and even though we've never met in person, I already learned a great deal from you.

Thank you to the whole Rizzoli team, who believed in me, gave me creative freedom, and allowed me to create the book I always wanted. Also, a special thanks to Rizzoli acquisition editor, Victorine Lamothe for believing in my idea and being an amazing supporter every step of the way.

A sincere thanks to Tori Ritchie for being a true mentor and teacher. I don't think this book would ever exist without your faith in me, your guidance, and your support.

To Jodi Liano and Chef Kirsten Goldberg from the San Francisco Cooking School. Thanks for making me a better cook and always rooting for me, even when I doubt myself.

To all of the amazing recipe testers who supported *Budmo!* on such an early stage. Your feedback made this cookbook so much better. Thank you.

I'd like to thank my partner in crime Halia Halavurta. We've already hosted countless pop-ups together, and we still have many more ahead of us. Also, your honey cake will always be my favorite dessert.

Finally, to my husband Sasha, whom I love so much that words can't express it. I dedicate this book to you!

Index

About the author

Anna Voloshyna was born and raised in Ukraine and lived there for twenty years before moving to the United States. After coming to the Bay Area, Anna started working as a food photographer and stylist, helping chefs and culinary brands tell their stories through her camera lens. After numerous photoshoots and exciting cooking endeavors, Anna was finally offered a chance to unveil her own food-making talents through hosting Eastern European pop-up dinners. Her Georgian *khachapuri* nights and Ukrainian *varenyky* feasts became a delicious sensation in the San Francisco culinary community. Now Anna's goal is to make people fall in love with Eastern European food through every little Ukrainian dumpling, fluffy garlic *pampushki*, and every single bowl of luscious borscht you'll cook from this book. Find Anna on Instagram **@annavoloshynacooks**.

Budmo!
Recipes from a Ukranian Kitchen

First published in the United States of America in 2022 by
Rizzoli International Publications, Inc.
300 Park Avenue South
New York, NY 10010
www.rizzoliusa.com

Publisher: Charles Miers
Editor: Victorine Lamothe
Production Manager: Kaija Markoe
Managing Editor: Lynn Scrabis

Editorial Packaging and Design: Leslie Jonath and Debbie Berne,
Connected Dots Media

Photographs on pages 14, 24, 61, 82, 99, 154, 188, 218, 220 by
Maria Boguslav. All other photographs by the author.

Printed in China

2022 2023 2024 2025 / 10 9 8 7 6 5 4 3 2 1

ISBN: 978-0-8478-7256-5
Library of Congress Control Number: 2022931455

Visit us online:
Facebook.com/RizzoliNewYork
Twitter: @Rizzoli_Books
Instagram.com/RizzoliBooks
Pinterest.com/RizzoliBooks
Youtube.com/user/RizzoliNY
Issuu.com/Rizzoli